Write to Win

The Ultimate Copywriting Handbook

Dana Hamilton

Table of Contents

Dedication

To my dearest daughters, Emily and Elise,

You are my greatest inspiration and a constant reminder that creativity, curiosity, and kindness can change the world. This book is for you—no matter where life takes you, I want you to know that your words carry power, your ideas matter, and your unique voice can shape the future. May you always chase your dreams, embrace learning, and never doubt the impact you can make.

With all my love,

Mom

Introduction

How do you make your voice stand out in a crowded digital landscape, where everyone is vying for attention and where the next big idea spreads like wildfire? Imagine a small, family-owned bakery nestled in a bustling city. It struggled to get clients for years, competing against larger chains with massive advertising budgets. It wasn't until they leveraged the power of storytelling that their fortunes changed. The bakery connected with its audience by sharing the heartwarming story of how Grandma's cherished recipes were lovingly crafted by her grandchildren and served fresh every day. Through its social media content and advertisements, the bakery didn't just sell bread and pastries; it shared a meaningful story with its customers. This story was rooted in family and tradition. Grandma's recipes were more than just a list of ingredients; they represented love, care, and generations of baking. The bakery's unique approach was to tell customers about the heartwarming journey of how these recipes came to life each day. Sales soared as customers felt drawn not just to delicious goods but to the story behind them. This example demonstrates the transformative power of persuasive writing—an essential skill for marketers, business owners, and content creators in today's landscape.

Persuasive writing, often referred to as copywriting, involves skillfully arranging words in a way that resonates deeply with your audience and forging connections to inspire them to take action. It's not merely about selling; it's about engaging people on an emotional level, offering solutions that respond to their desires and needs. In essence, every headline you see, every email subject line that catches your eye, and every product description that makes you stop scrolling has been tailored with the art of persuasion in mind.

So, what exactly is copywriting, and why has it become indispensable across various fields? At its core, copywriting is the practice of writing text for advertising or marketing. The text, known as "copy," is written content that aims to increase brand awareness and ultimately persuade a person or group to take a particular action. Whether it's buying a product, clicking on a link, or subscribing to a service, effective copywriting taps into human psychology and aligns with our intrinsic motivations.

Within this book, we will dive deep into the mechanics of what makes copywriting so powerful. We'll explore how understanding audience psychology can transform a mundane message into a magnetic one. You'll learn the craft of developing compelling messages that don't just inform but also inspire and ignite change. We will demystify the art of storytelling in copywriting—an ancient technique still relevant and potent in today's digital era. Storytelling doesn't just make your content appealing; it makes it memorable.

Who stands to gain the most from mastering these skills? Whether you're a seasoned marketer looking to refine your strategies, a business owner aiming to articulate your value propositions clearly, or a content creator eager to enhance the quality of your work, this book is your guide. It covers the foundational skills to build a successful copywriting business and attract clients with impactful and persuasive writing. Similarly, sales professionals will find the insights necessary to compose compelling messages that lead directly to conversions.

Here's what to keep in mind throughout this journey: Knowledge alone is not enough—it calls for application. Each chapter comes with practical exercises designed to help you implement what you've learned immediately. By actively engaging with the material, you'll transition from theory to practice, witnessing firsthand how these techniques can elevate your content and communication.

By the time you reach the final pages, my hope is that you will not only understand the principles of effective copywriting but will also have transformed your approach to writing altogether. Mastering persuasive writing isn't just about achieving professional success—it enables personal growth, too. It empowers you to communicate more effectively, influence positively, and realize both your personal and professional aspirations.

As you turn the page to begin this exploration into the world of persuasive copywriting, remember the humble bakery that transformed its fate through the power of story. Your journey might start here between these pages, but its impact could ripple far beyond—a shift in strategy, a boost in confidence, and a new chapter in your career. Embrace the challenge, apply yourself diligently, and watch as your words work wonders, shaping destinies and driving results. Welcome to the art of copywriting; let's uncover the power of words to make a positive impact on more lives and transform your business, career, and life!

Chapter 1:

Cultivating the Core Mindset Traits

Have you ever wondered what mindset traits set the most successful copywriters apart? In this chapter, you'll discover three core traits—empathy, curiosity, and creativity—that are essential for crafting persuasive and impactful writing. These qualities are valuable tools for creating messages that truly resonate with your audience. As we explore these characteristics, you'll learn how they intertwine to enhance your ability to connect with readers on a deeper emotional level, paving the way for successful communication.

Empathy takes center stage as we uncover its power to transform interactions by aligning our messages with our audience's emotions. You'll learn to harness this understanding to move beyond surface connections and uncover underlying needs and motivations. Next, we will delve into your creative potential, which involves embracing unique ideas and innovative approaches. Finally, we'll examine curiosity, a trait that fuels your drive to explore new possibilities and adapt your writing to ever-evolving trends.

Understanding Audience Needs

Through Empathy

Empathy in copywriting goes beyond mere words; it's about truly understanding your audience's motivations and needs. At its core, empathy allows you to step into the shoes of your readers, providing insights that lead to crafting messages that resonate deeply with them. Through the power of emotion-driven content, you can create a narrative that not only captures attention but also engages the heart and mind.

Building Emotional Connections

The secret to building emotional connections lies in how well you can evoke feelings within your audience. People often make decisions based on emotions and subsequently justify them with logic (Ahmad, 2023). It means that if you instill emotions such as joy, trust, or even frustration in your copy, it will likely hook your readers. For instance, highlighting relatable stories or situations can stir emotions like nostalgia or inspiration, drawing your readers in on a personal level.

Moreover, a relatable message doesn't just tell—it connects by reflecting shared values or emotions. Have you noticed how effective advertisements evoke childhood nostalgia or champion real-life testimonials? These strategies work because they speak to universal human experiences, drawing readers in and making them feel seen and understood. To achieve this, storytellers often weave in everyday scenarios or challenges that mirror those faced by their audience, making the content not only engaging but also relevant.

Additionally, understanding your audience's emotions helps to tailor the tone and style of your messaging to meet their needs. If audience research indicates that your readership is typically stressed, adopting a soothing, reassuring tone can be highly effective. Conversely, an energetic, upbeat approach might resonate better if they're seeking excitement or innovation. This adaptability is essential: the same message delivered with different emotional tones will often yield very different results.

Identifying Pain Points

Addressing pain points is another essential aspect that reinforces the importance of empathy. It's not enough to know what your audience desires; understanding their struggles and frustrations is key to offering meaningful and valuable solutions (Dogli Wilberforce, 2023). Imagine you're speaking directly to an individual who feels overwhelmed by choices in a crowded marketplace. Your task is to articulate their unspoken issues clearly while presenting your product or service as the remedy they didn't realize they needed. This is where empathy shines –

in the capability to resonate with unsaid fears and transform them into opportunities for positive change.

By acknowledging the challenges or frustrations consumers face, you position yourself as allies who understand and are eager to help. This approach can greatly enhance trust and rapport. For instance, a company selling ergonomic office chairs might acknowledge the common discomfort of long hours spent sitting, then present their product as a solution designed with customer comfort in mind. This addresses a practical need *and* shows empathy—an understanding of what customers endure daily.

Active Listening

Adopting active listening skills is beneficial to truly understand your audience and refine your messaging strategy. In a world where feedback is instant and critiques are readily available, welcoming this input can elevate the effectiveness of your communication. Engaging with your audience through surveys, social media interactions, or direct feedback sessions offers a wealth of information. It not only helps you fine-tune your approach but also demonstrates to your audience that their voices are valued and heard. This reciprocal flow of communication nurtures loyalty and lets you stay attuned to their evolving needs and preferences (Wells, 2023).

What's more, open dialogue further aids in refining your messaging. When audiences feel they are part of a conversation rather than passive recipients of information, they are more likely to engage. Encouraging feedback through surveys, social media interactions, and direct communications can provide a continuous stream of useful information. Once you establish this dialogue, it becomes easier to enhance your approach, ensuring your messages are not just reaching people but are impactful and meaningful. This ongoing exchange helps build stronger relationships, as your audience feels heard and valued.

Personas and Segmentation

Creating detailed audience personas is a strategic tool for visualizing target segments, allowing you to customize your messages more precisely. This strategy starts with building comprehensive profiles that encompass demographics, behaviors, and aspirations as a starting point to craft messages that speak directly to each segment's unique needs (Ajao, 2023). This segmentation process makes it possible for you to connect with different subsets of your audience effectively, ensuring that each message hits home with accuracy and relevance. Most importantly, developing personas requires genuine empathy to grasp the diversity within your audience and deliver consistency in your brand's voice.

Segmentation involves dividing your broader audience into smaller, more defined groups based on shared characteristics such as demographics, behaviors, or preferences (Rao, 2023). By doing this, you can personalize your messages to suit each group's unique needs and interests. For example, younger audiences might prefer messaging that is visually engaging and accessible via social media, while older segments may appreciate more detailed information delivered through traditional channels like newsletters. This personalized approach ensures that your communication efforts are objective, which contributes to the impact of your campaigns without wasting resources on generic messages that appeal to everyone except your target audience.

Effective segmentation requires careful research and analysis. You need to gather data from various sources, including customer feedback, analytics, and market studies, to create profiles or personas that accurately reflect your audience's traits. These personas serve as detailed representations of your ideal customers and guide the development of customized messages. The beauty of personas is that they bring your audience to life, allowing you to craft messages that resonate on a personal level. Tailoring messages based on these personas dramatically improves engagement rates because your audience sees themselves in the content, making it more relatable and compelling.

In today's fast-paced digital landscape, where messages are overwhelming and attention spans are short, standing out requires more than just creativity. It demands a strategic approach to messaging that leverages audience feedback and precise segmentation. Workplace and external segmentation satisfy different communication needs and aid in targeting messages effectively. Likewise, revisiting and refining audience segments continuously ensures that your communication remains relevant and impactful (Dutta, 2023). By setting clear metrics such as engagement and conversion rates, you can assess and adapt your strategies to meet changing audience dynamics.

Understanding your audience holistically is vital to formulating impactful copy. Empathy extends beyond acknowledging surface-level emotions; it's about diving deeper into understanding the context behind those feelings. This involves conducting thorough audience research to uncover insights that inform your creative and strategic direction. Techniques such as empathy mapping and analyzing customer journeys allow you to visualize emotional experiences at every touchpoint, giving you a clearer picture of how to address their needs and challenges.

Incorporating empathy into your copy isn't a one-size-fits-all solution; it's a nuanced skill that requires practice and mindfulness. By feeling as you write and aligning with your reader's emotions, you create genuine and persuasive content. Remember that empathy isn't merely about identifying problems but presenting solutions in a way that resonates authentically with your audience.

Cultivating Curiosity to Craft Compelling Copy

Being curious can significantly boost your copywriting skills in several ways. This innate curiosity drives you to ask questions, seek answers, and discover new perspectives, which ultimately enhances your ability to create engaging and relatable content.

Research Skills

One vital aspect of research is understanding different audience preferences. Knowing your audience allows you to tailor your content to meet their needs. You can gather this knowledge through surveys, social media polls, or simply by engaging with your audience in relevant forums. This direct interaction can provide a wealth of information about what interests your readers most (Copywriting.org, 2023).

Understanding trends is equally important. Trends can shape the topics you choose to write about. You can stay ahead of the curve by keeping an eye on industry news and assessing shifts in public interest. For instance, if plant-based diets are gaining popularity, you could delve into their benefits and draw comparisons between various diets. This kind of timely content attracts attention and positions you as a knowledgeable source within your niche.

Stay open to new information and viewpoints throughout the research process. Sometimes, you may find that your initial understanding of a topic shifts as you gather more data. Be willing to adapt your ideas and arguments as needed. Embracing such a mindset can lead to a better understanding of your audience,

Understanding Audience's Needs

Imagine stepping into your audience's shoes—what if you could truly understand their wants and needs? This is where curiosity becomes your best ally! By embracing a curious mindset, you're inspired to ask insightful questions that reveal what matters to your audience (Copywriting.org, 2023). This helps you connect on a deeper level and empowers you to craft messages that resonate profoundly with them. Start by researching your audience to understand their interests and preferences. What entertains them? What are their pain points? From here, brainstorm ideas that align with these insights. Mind mapping can be helpful in generating and organizing thoughts. Once ideas flow, evaluate them critically, considering both their uniqueness and relevance to brand messaging. When you know exactly what they're looking for, your copy becomes a conversation, guiding them toward solutions that feel personalized and relevant.

Creative Thinking

Curiosity is like a spark that ignites your creative thinking, pushing you to explore new ideas and perspectives. When you're curious, you're not just sticking to the usual ways of doing things; instead, you're eager to dig deeper and consider different angles. This mindset encourages you to think outside the box, which is essential for crafting unique and compelling copy (Copywriting.org, 2023b). It might inspire you to experiment with fresh metaphors, discover unexpected connections, or approach topics from a whole new angle. As a result, your writing not only stands out but also captures your audience's attention in a way that resonates with them.

Experimentation

Experimentation is a crucial part of growing as a copywriter. When you're curious, you're more inclined to try out different copy formats, styles, and calls to action, which opens the door to discovering what truly works for your audience (Farber, 2020). Maybe you'll play with a conversational tone in one piece, try a more formal approach in another, or test out catchy headlines versus straightforward ones. Each time you experiment, you learn something new about what resonates with your readers, helping you refine your skills and build your confidence. Plus, these experiments can lead to unexpected breakthroughs that make your writing even more compelling.

Harnessing Creativity for Unique Messaging

In today's bustling marketplace, creativity in copywriting is more than just a skill; it's a necessity. As brands vie for consumer attention, distinctive messaging becomes the beacon that draws an audience. Hence, creativity will make your copy stand out.

Innovative Approaches

The first step in instilling creativity in copywriting is adopting fresh perspectives. This means going beyond conventional ideas and tapping into unique viewpoints that appeal to the target audience. It's about asking questions like, "What hasn't been said before?" or "How can we say this differently?" Challenging traditional narratives can open the door to originality (Farber, 2020). For instance, take the concept of humor, which can provide an unexpected twist that captures attention when tastefully integrated into copy. In addition to that, innovative copy might also play on words or introduce surprising contrasts that make the reader pause and think. Developing this knack requires curiosity, open-mindedness, and a keen observation of cultural trends.

Storytelling Techniques

Beyond innovation lies the art of storytelling—a powerful tool to transform mundane information into compelling narratives. Storytelling in copywriting is not just about recounting events but weaving them in a way that connects emotionally with the audience. A good story grabs attention by creating a vivid picture that sticks in the mind long after the reading is done. Imagine introducing a narrative that takes readers on a journey—one that illustrates a problem and culminates in a satisfying resolution provided by your product or service. Stories invite audiences to immerse themselves deeply through characters or relatable scenarios, making the message memorable and impactful (Slade, 2023). Thus, narratives are an excellent strategy to convey even complex ideas simply yet engagingly.

Visual and Conceptual Imagery

You can incorporate visual and conceptual imagery to enhance reader engagement and retention. Words have the power to paint pictures in the mind (Brosch, 2018). When writing copy, envision the images your words evoke. For example, describing a product's refreshing nature might compare its effect to a cool breeze on a hot summer day. Such imagery gives life to text and ignites the imagination. Visual metaphors can also serve as bridges connecting abstract concepts with tangible experiences, making messages clearer and more impactful. The goal is to enable readers to "see" what you mean, thereby deepening their connection to the content.

Images or videos that accompany written content should align with the emotional tone of the message. They can amplify feelings of joy, urgency, or comfort and help bring the narrative to life. Visual aids serve as a bridge between the writer's intentions and the audience's perceptions, enhancing overall engagement.

Experimentation With Language

Experimentation with language involves playing with syntax, rhythm, and word choice to craft an inviting and compelling read. Language is a versatile tool—how it's wielded can significantly influence a message's appeal (Ud-deen, 2020). Consider the impact of rhythm in phrases; a perfectly timed sentence can resonate like a catchy tune. Alliteration or repetition adds a lyrical quality that makes text enjoyable to read and easy to remember. Jargon-free and straightforward language ensures clarity and invites a broad audience to relate and respond. Think of how some famous slogans manage to say so much with so few words—their power often resides in carefully chosen expressions that strike emotional chords while communicating core ideas efficiently.

Also, it's important to acknowledge the strategic use of language in forming these emotional bonds. Word choice can significantly impact how a message is received. Crafting sentences with carefully chosen adjectives and inclusive language can make readers feel part of a community rather than just a target market. For instance, using inclusive pronouns can create a sense of belonging and reinforce the idea that the brand and its customers are on this journey together.

Summary and Reflections

In this chapter, we looked into the vital role that empathy, curiosity, and creativity play in successful copywriting. These traits allow copywriters to connect meaningfully with their audience by understanding and addressing their needs and emotions. We also explored how empathy helps you see through your audience's eyes, bridging the gap between their challenges and your solutions. Additionally, actively listening and crafting messages that resonate personally is a smart way to create a winning copy and transform ordinary communication into a nurturing dialogue. This approach not only builds trust but also ensures your audience feels valued and heard.

Equally important is harnessing creativity to differentiate your messaging. In a world full of competing voices, standing out requires creative strategies that combine storytelling, visual imagery, and innovative language. Together, these elements form a cohesive strategy, empowering you to craft compelling narratives that foster loyalty, drive conversions, and elevate your brands above the rest.

Chapter 2:

Understanding Your Audience

This chapter invites you to embark on a journey of discovery—learning about your target market's desires, needs, and pain points. Imagine unlocking the key to their minds and hearts, allowing you to speak directly to what matters most to them. As you dive deeper, you'll realize that this understanding is not merely an added value but a fundamental pillar in any effective marketing strategy.

As you navigate this chapter, you will explore insightful strategies for identifying and analyzing your target audience's characteristics and behaviors. You'll also learn how to conduct thorough research to unveil not only demographic details but also psychographic insights that reveal motivations and interests. The chapter will guide you on techniques like surveys and interviews for gathering valuable data, emphasizing the importance of embracing feedback and complaints as opportunities for growth. Additionally, we'll uncover the significance of competitor analysis and how it can illuminate areas where your brand can stand out. Moreover, you'll discover how leveraging online tools and analytics can equip you with concrete data to inform your content direction.

Research Audience Needs, Desires, and Pain Points

Understanding what genuinely motivates your audience is vital to crafting strategic and impactful marketing content. Gaining a clear perspective on their needs, desires, and frustrations can help you tailor your message to resonate with them on a deeper level.

Surveys and Interviews

Using surveys and interviews is invaluable to gather firsthand information about your audience. Surveys allow you to reach a broader demographic quickly, providing statistical data that can reveal overarching trends within your audience. Interviews, on the other hand, offer qualitative insights, allowing you to delve deeper into individual experiences and preferences. A well-designed survey or interview can uncover specific details about your audience's needs and preferences. These insights serve as a reference for creating your content strategy, ensuring it aligns with what your audience values most.

When designing surveys or interviews, make sure that questions are clear, concise, and geared towards eliciting detailed responses that will inform your content strategy (Aw, 2024). Use open-ended questions to gain nuanced insights and closed questions for quantitative analysis. Regularly review and refine your questions based on the results to continuously improve the quality of the data you gather.

Feedback and Complaints

Analyzing feedback and complaints is a simple method for understanding your audience's pain points. Feedback from various channels—whether comments on social media, emails, or direct conversations—provides authentic insights into what your audience appreciates or finds lacking (Maku Seun, 2024). Complaints can be particularly enlightening, as they highlight areas where expectations are not being met. When you address these issues directly in your content, you demonstrate empathy and commitment to improvement, which can enhance audience trust and loyalty.

When analyzing feedback and complaints, categorize and quantify the insights. Look for patterns in the data to identify recurring themes or issues. This approach allows you to prioritize the most significant concerns to address in your content. Don't forget to respond promptly to feedback, showing your audience that their opinions are valued and acted upon.

Competitor Analysis

Conducting a competitor analysis further refines your research because examining your competitors' strategies helps to understand how similar audiences respond to them. This involves reviewing their content, identifying successful tactics, and noting any gaps they might have left unaddressed. Understanding competitor strengths and weaknesses provides opportunities for differentiation, giving you the chance to position your brand uniquely (Doan, 2023). For instance, if your competitors focus heavily on one aspect of service but neglect another, you can fill that gap with tailored content that meets those unserved needs.

Keep in mind that competitor analysis requires ongoing monitoring of their content and audience interactions. Identify what formats—like blogs, videos, or infographics—they use effectively and note any shortcomings. Also, regularly assess how their audience engages with their content, paying attention to likes, shares, and comments. This analysis informs your strategy and helps you refine your tone and style to better suit your audience.

Online Tools

Leveraging online tools like Google Trends can provide valuable data regarding the interests and behaviors of your target audience. Such tools facilitate a clear understanding of search trends and general interest levels over time, reflecting what topics are gaining traction among your audience (Breaux, 2021).

In practice, you can integrate data from platforms such as Google Analytics with insights from Google Trends to get a comprehensive picture of your audience's interests. These tools can help identify spikes in interest related to specific keywords or topics, guiding you on when to publish content for maximum impact. Continuously adapting to these insights ensures your strategy remains aligned with evolving audience preferences. Armed with this knowledge, you can craft content that taps into current interests and anticipates future trends.

Create Detailed Buyer Personas

In today's dynamic marketplace, understanding your audience goes beyond just knowing who they are. Crafting vibrant profiles of your ideal customers is essential in delivering tailored marketing messages that resonate. Detailed buyer personas tap into the target demographics of your audience, including their preferences, pain points, and aspirations. This practice results in tailored marketing messages that resonate, engage, and inspire action.

Key Demographics

To build comprehensive customer profiles, start by defining key demographics. These are the measurable characteristics of your audience, like age, gender, and income. Imagine a clothing brand targeting young adults aged 18-24. Here, the age group acts as a solid foundation upon which further attributes are built. Demographics help you grasp the concrete aspects of your audience, enabling more precise targeting in your campaigns. Analyzing these concrete aspects helps to determine the needs and preferences of different segments within your target market. This understanding allows for more precise targeting in your campaigns, ensuring that your messages reach the right people at the right time.

Psychographics

Psychographics encompass the psychological aspects of consumers—such as motivations, values, attitudes, and lifestyle choices—that influence their buying decisions (Chow, 2022). Understanding these factors allows you to predict not only what your customers will buy but also why they make those purchases. Once you grasp the reasons behind their decisions, you can create more personalized strategies to reach them: From the way you build your offer to the manner you advertise it, all your marketing efforts are aligned with their specific aspirations and values. Consequently, you have more chance to succeed while the risk of failure is reduced.

For instance, consider a tech company selling health-focused smartwatches. Beyond targeting health-conscious individuals (a demographic aspect), understanding the deeper motivations, such as a desire for self-improvement or status, can refine how you position your product. Acknowledging these psychographics leads to connecting with customers on an emotional level, driving a stronger call to action. Ultimately, leveraging psychographics can transform marketing strategies, making them more relevant and impactful in the eyes of your customers.

Persona Narratives

Creating persona narratives is a powerful method for humanizing and relating to your audience's needs. A persona narrative transforms static data into a story that embodies the typical experiences and challenges faced by a segment of your audience (Copywriting.org, 2023b). For example, it might personify "Anna," a 35-year-old working mother who juggles a busy schedule but is equally committed to maintaining a healthy lifestyle. By crafting her story, marketers can envision real-world scenarios and produce content that speaks directly to Anna's unique needs and aspirations.

When drafting these narratives, consider detailing how your product or service fits into their day-to-day life. Ask yourself the following questions: What problems does it solve? How does it enhance their personal or professional journey? The goal is to ensure that your audience can see themselves in these narratives. This creates a sense of connection and understanding, which reinforces their bond with your brand. This approach enhances brand loyalty and encourages potential customers to imagine a more fulfilling and better life with your product or service as an essential part of it.

Case Studies

Real-world examples of effective buyer personas underscore the impact these profiles can have. A notable case is a beauty brand that adapted its messaging after unveiling a persona representing ethical consumers passionate about sustainability. Rather than merely promoting product features, the brand emphasized its eco-friendly initiatives and partnerships with environmental organizations. This shift attracted a new wave of loyal customers who identified deeply with these values.

So, where should you begin with creating these impactful buyer personas? Start with thorough research. Collect data from a variety of sources, such as surveys, focus groups, and direct customer interviews. Next, examine existing customer feedback and sales data to unearth trends that form the core attributes of your personas. Don't shy away from utilizing digital tools like online analytics and social media listening to gain additional insights into consumer behavior and preferences. As you collect this data, look for patterns that indicate shared desires, pain points, and aspirations among your audience. These insights will become the building blocks of your personas, providing clarity and direction for your marketing strategies.

Once you've defined your groups, create profiles that encapsulate both the demographics and psychographics. Give each persona a name and a backstory, identifying their goals, challenges, and how your business can address their needs. Ensure that these profiles are accessible and understandable, serving as a living document referenced throughout your marketing efforts. Finally, remember that the process of defining your audience is continuous. Consumer preferences and markets evolve, so revisit and refine your personas regularly to maintain relevance and effectiveness.

Develop Creative Ideas for Engaging Content

Connecting your understanding of an audience to effective content ideas is a cornerstone of impactful marketing strategies. Let's dive into how you can effectively brainstorm and implement diverse content ideas that resonate with your target audience.

Brainstorming Techniques

A fruitful brainstorming session is the first step toward creating engaging content. One of the best techniques to employ during these sessions is mind mapping. Mind mapping allows you to visualize connections between different ideas, facilitating the generation of creative concepts (Atlassian, n.d.). It's a simple yet powerful method to encourage free thinking while ensuring all ideas are connected and focused on your audience's needs. This technique involves writing down a central topic, like a specific product or service, and branching out into related themes, questions, or pain points that your audience might have. Mind mapping fosters comprehensive discussion and helps uncover new ideas that could be transformed into compelling content.

Content Formats

As you brainstorm, it's essential not to limit yourself to one type of content format. Different audiences have varied preferences for consuming information. Therefore, exploring multiple content formats—such as blogs, videos, infographics, and podcasts—can be beneficial. Blogs are great for discussing in-depth topics, offering insights, and building engagement through comments and shares. Videos, on the other hand, offer a dynamic way to capture attention, which is especially useful for demonstrating products or sharing quick tutorials. Infographics simplify complex information, making it digestible and easy to share. Podcasts provide an avenue for extended discussions and personal storytelling. You cater to different segments of your audience, ensuring wider reach and more profound impact with a diversity of content types.

Trends and Popular Culture

Trends and popular culture offer a treasure trove of topics to extract content ideas from. Aligning your content with current trends can significantly boost its relevance and shareability (Breaux, 2021). Stay updated on trending topics within your industry and broader cultural movements to achieve this. Social media platforms and tools like Google Trends can help you monitor what's capturing the public's attention. For instance, if sustainability is gaining traction among your audience, creating content that highlights eco-friendly practices could engage them powerfully. When appropriate, incorporating references from popular culture, like movie dialogues or viral memes, adds a relatable touch that can make your content more engaging.

User-Generated Content

Incorporating user-generated content (UGC) in your strategy is a fantastic way to foster community engagement while simultaneously understanding your audience better. UGC involves inviting your audience members to contribute content related to your brand, such as reviews, photos, or experiences (Oladipo, 2022). This approach builds a sense of community and provides authentic content that potential customers find credible. Encourage participation through themed challenges or contests on social media, perhaps by using branded hashtags. Highlighting and rewarding the best submissions can motivate continued engagement. Campaigns driven by UGC often succeed in creating a dialogue around your brand, leading to increased loyalty and engagement.

Analyze Competitor Strategies

One effective strategy for better understanding your audience is to learn from your competitors. This practice can provide valuable insights into refining your engagement tactics and better connecting with your target market.

Identifying Gaps

This process involves analyzing where competitors might be underperforming or leaving niches unaddressed. For instance, if a competing brand has a strong online presence but weak customer service, this gap presents an opportunity for you to shine by offering superior customer interactions. Recognizing such weaknesses can help you position your brand more favorably, appealing to aspects of the audience's needs that others overlook. Moreover, examining content types and channels they neglect can help you reach untapped audience segments. Introducing missing content formats like video tutorials or interactive polls could set you apart in saturated markets.

Decoding Competitors' Messaging

Understanding competitor messaging is also vital to ensuring your communication aligns with audience expectations. Competitors who speak effectively to your shared audience offer a blueprint for what works. Analyzing their language, tone, and message structure can guide you in shaping your approach (Bray, 2022). For example, if a rival company uses humor successfully to engage a young demographic, incorporating a similar playful style into your messaging could resonate well without directly copying. It's about adopting proven techniques while infusing your unique brand voice. When you mirror the messaging style that already captivates the audience, you stand a better chance of retaining their attention and fostering loyalty.

Studying Successful Tactics

You can also pay attention to how competitors engage with their audience and adjust your tone accordingly. This involves a deep dive into how they interact with audiences on various platforms—be it through direct communication, social media posts, or email newsletters. Observing the frequency and style of these interactions provides insight into what resonates with the audience. For instance, consistent, friendly updates may encourage frequent engagement, while authoritative, informative pieces might establish credibility. Tailoring your tone to match or exceed these standards ensures your brand remains relatable and trustworthy. Take note of how open or formal competitors are in their interactions and consider whether those approaches meet your audience's preferences (Bray, 2022).

Paying Attention to Audience's Reaction

Moreover, observing audience reactions to competitor campaigns offers strategic insights that can shape your initiatives. Pay close attention to which campaigns elicit positive responses and why. Perhaps a competitor's behind-the-scenes content garners high engagement due to its transparency and authenticity, suggesting that your audience values honesty and openness. On the flip side, negative feedback on certain campaigns can be equally enlightening, teaching you what to avoid in your efforts. Learning from their successes and failures allows you to craft campaigns that are not only innovative but also deeply attuned to audience desires.

To execute this analysis effectively without overextending resources, focus on key performance metrics that reflect engagement success. These include engagement rates, sharing frequencies, and sentiment expressed in reviews and comments. Start with competitors closely aligned with your market scope, then expand to include broader industry leaders and emerging challengers as needed. Having a structured method to capture and review this data regularly provides clarity on shifting trends and audience preferences. Maintaining a meticulous record of observations will ensure you can adapt swiftly to changes in the market landscape, staying ahead of competitors in addressing the evolving needs of your audience.

Utilize Online Analytical Tools

In the digital age, successful marketing requires understanding your audience. One powerful way to achieve this is by harnessing online data to inform precise targeting and messaging.

Google Trends

Google Trends is an invaluable resource for obtaining quantifiable data about what captivates audiences worldwide. This tool reveals where specific search terms are most popular geographically, allowing marketers to customize content for different regions. This geographic insight helps uncover new markets that could be untapped by competitors, presenting opportunities for niche topics. Moreover, Google Trends provides related queries and topics, offering a comprehensive view of consumer interest. Identifying these related elements can aid in discovering long-tail keywords and emerging trends within your industry to create highly relevant and engaging content. Using this tool effectively can significantly boost the visibility of your copy, making your copy relevant to your target audience (Patel, 2022).

Search Behaviors

Beyond Google Trends, analyzing search behaviors allows marketers to forecast emerging trends and fine-tune their content strategies accordingly. Monitoring search patterns over time offers insights into changing consumer preferences and potential shifts in demand. This foreknowledge enables brands to stay ahead of the curve, providing timely content that connects with their audience. To do so, evaluate seasonal trends and spikes around specific events or holidays before planning your content calendar. This proactive approach ensures that high-quality, relevant content is ready when demand peaks, optimizing chances for organic ranking and increased engagement.

User Analytics

Another essential strategy involves employing user analytics to tailor messages more accurately to specific audience segments. You can segment your audience through analytic platforms based on demographics, interests, and online behaviors. These insights allow for the creation of personalized messages that speak directly to the needs and desires of each segment. For example, understanding which types of content perform best with specific demographics can guide future content creation, making it more resonant and compelling. Personalized marketing increases engagement and fosters stronger relationships between brands and consumers, driving customer loyalty and conversions.

Data-Driven Insights

Continuously adapting content strategies based on data-driven insights is vital in maintaining relevance and effectiveness. Make it a habit to review key metrics and performance data to identify areas for improvement and highlight emerging trends. This agile approach allows you to pivot strategies as needed, keeping content fresh and aligned with audience expectations (Patel, 2022). The goal is to ensure your brand remains at the forefront of customer engagement.

Summary and Reflections

This chapter empowers you to craft copy that truly resonates with your audience. From utilizing surveys and interviews to gain qualitative insights to analyzing feedback and complaints to pinpoint pain points, you've learned how to gather comprehensive data about your target audience. Understanding competitor strategies and leveraging online tools further enhances your grasp on crafting relevant content. These approaches collectively equip you with the knowledge to capture your audience's attention while building lasting engagement.

Now, with detailed buyer personas in hand, you're well-positioned to align your messaging with consumer motivations and values. Crafting compelling narratives based on customer demographics and psychographics allows you to connect with your audience on a personal level, ensuring your content speaks directly to their needs and aspirations. This strategic understanding strengthens your marketing efforts and fosters loyalty and trust, driving sustained business success.

Chapter 3:

Crafting Compelling Headlines

Crafting compelling headlines is essential to capture attention and motivate clicks. These brief yet powerful phrases are content gatekeepers, capable of drawing in a curious audience or leaving them scrolling past without a second thought. Well-crafted headlines spark curiosity and set the tone for the entire interaction with your audience. They act as the initial handshake, inviting readers into the depth and breadth of what lies beyond.

In this chapter, we'll learn the best strategies for writing those captivating headlines that hook your audience. Then, we'll explore the tactics of using benefit-oriented language and problem-solving techniques to make relevant headlines. We'll also discuss the role of incentives and clarity in encouraging immediate engagement, ensuring your message isn't lost in clever wordplay. From understanding the subtle nuances of human psychology to implementing structured guidelines for consistency, this chapter offers a comprehensive toolkit for elevating your headline crafting skills.

Use Headlines That Promise a Benefit or Solve a Problem

Crafting compelling headlines requires a deep understanding of the audience's needs. Effective headlines do more than just grab attention; they directly address and fulfill these needs, creating a bridge between product and potential customer. Let's explore key strategies involved in crafting such impactful headlines.

Benefit-Oriented Headlines

First and foremost, a headline should clearly communicate the specific benefits of a product or service. Highlighting these advantages helps capture readers' attention and build a sense of anticipation, making them feel that their specific needs and desires are considered and will be addressed. This approach encourages engagement by making readers feel that their needs will be met.

When writing headlines, prioritize clarity and specificity to ensure that your audience quickly grasps the primary advantage you offer. They must easily understand what your offer can do for them, whether it's improving their health, boosting their productivity, or adopting new habits about money. The more precise your headline is, the more effective it is. This method is invaluable for one simple reason: People are more inclined to engage with content that speaks directly to their personal gain.

Problem-Solving Headlines

Next, be willing to solve problems through your headlines. Here's why: Humans are naturally drawn to solutions, especially when experiencing frustration or inconvenience. You can forge an immediate connection by articulating a challenge your audience faces and hinting at a solution. Imagine a headline such as "Struggling With Time Management? Discover Strategies That Work to Accomplish All Your Tasks." This structure acknowledges a common problem—time management—and promises guidance toward solutions (Jamal, 2024). Such headlines work because they are oriented on the reader's desire to overcome obstacles, positioning your content as a helpful resource.

When incorporating problem-solving elements, remember to strike a balance between emphasizing the issue and suggesting a solution. Avoid dwelling too much on negative aspects, as this may deter potential customers. Instead, position your product or service as a seamless transition from the problem stage to the solution phase.

Incentives for Action

Words like "free," "limited," or "exclusive" generate a sense of urgency and exclusivity. They suggest that the opportunity presented is not only valuable but also scarce, prompting readers to act swiftly to avoid missing out (Forbes, 2021). A headline stating "Unlock Free Access to Premium Content Today" leverages this tactic effectively. The promise of something beneficial without cost can motivate clicks and conversions. However, ensuring that these incentives are genuine and deliver on their commitment to maintain trust with your audience is essential.

Misleading incentives can lead to a loss of credibility and hurt brand reputation. Therefore, while crafting headlines with incentives, align them closely with what your business can genuinely offer. Regularly update these headlines to reflect new offers or promotions to keep your content fresh and engaging.

Clarity Over Cleverness

While creativity is often celebrated in writing, clarity over cleverness is paramount in effective headline creation. Complex wordplay can sometimes obscure the core message and confuse readers, leading them to skip over your content entirely. Instead, opt for straightforward headlines that convey clear benefits. Consider the difference between "Revolutionize Your Lifestyle" and "Achieve a Healthier Lifestyle with Simple Changes." The latter immediately informs the reader of what they can expect. Hence, prioritizing transparency in your headlines ensures your audience understands exactly what you're offering, increasing the chances of meaningful engagement.

Guidelines

To harness these techniques effectively, start by identifying your target audience's primary needs and concerns. Use research and data-driven insights to understand these pain points deeply. Once identified, draft headlines that directly address these needs using benefit-oriented language. Ensure each headline includes a clear value proposition that distinguishes your offering from competitors. Use tools and methodologies like the AIDA framework—Attention, Interest, Desire, Action—to structure your headline's flow, beginning with capturing attention and concluding with a persuasive call to action (O'Connell, 2023).

Finally, embrace simplicity over complexity. Review your headlines critically, asking whether every word serves a purpose. Eliminate unnecessary jargon that might confuse or distract from the main message. Simplicity doesn't mean sacrificing quality—it means refining your message so it's easily digestible and memorable.

Test Different Headline Styles

In the realm of crafting compelling headlines, it's vital to explore the various styles that connect with audiences and test their effectiveness in grabbing attention.

Types of Headlines

There are different types of headlines; each style can be a powerful tool in your arsenal. Questions, for instance, provoke curiosity and invite readers to ponder answers. A headline like "Are You Making These Common Marketing Mistakes?" immediately engages the audience by challenging them to learn more. Similarly, list-based headlines such as "5 Tips to Boost Your Sales Today" offer a structured, digestible promise of valuable information, catering to readers who appreciate clarity and concise takeaways. Statements, on the other hand, can assert authority or make bold claims that compel readers to explore further, like "Why Your Business Needs a Strong Online Presence Now."

The Power of A/B Testing

A/B testing is an experimental method used to compare two versions of a webpage or element, such as a headline, to see which performs better (Grigat, 2022). By randomly assigning visitors to two groups and showing each group a different headline, you can gather data on metrics like click-through rates and time spent on the page. This approach helps identify which style echoes with your target audience, providing insights into their preferences and behaviors. For example, if a question-based headline consistently outperforms a list-based one, you have concrete evidence to direct your future content strategy.

Analyzing Audience Response

Data-driven decision-making allows you to refine your headline strategically. Analytics tools provide a detailed look at how audiences react to different headlines, tracking metrics like bounce rates, conversion rates, and social shares. When analyzing this data, you can uncover patterns that indicate what styles best capture interest and lead to desired actions. For instance, if analysis reveals that headlines focusing on benefits such as "Increase Your ROI by 30% With This Simple Change" result in higher engagement, it guides future headline development towards similar approaches.

Iterate and Improve

After collecting data and analyzing audience responses, the journey doesn't end there. The last step is to iterate and improve by encouraging experimentation and applying the findings from testing. It's important to cultivate a mindset of constant learning and adaptation to craft the perfect headline (Lee, 2023). Use the insights gained from A/B testing and audience analytics to tweak and experiment further with headline styles. Perhaps a slight modification, like altering a word or changing the order of elements, could significantly enhance engagement. In doing so, you create a feedback loop where each experiment informs the next, fostering ongoing improvement and innovation in headline creation.

To exemplify this iterative process, let's consider a scenario: Suppose a headline using a statement style underperforms compared to others. Instead of discarding it outright, look at what aspects might be optimized. Is the wording too generic, or does it lack urgency? Experiment with variations that address these areas. Maybe incorporate elements from successful headlines, such as numbers or emotionally charged adjectives, to boost its appeal. Through this trial-and-error method, your headlines become not only attention-grabby but also strategically aligned with audience preferences and brand objectives.

A Test-And-Learn Process

A test-and-learn approach is undoubtedly the most effective strategy for enhancing the performance of your headlines, allowing for continual experimentation and refinement. Monitor the results of your various headline iterations to identify valuable insights into what resonates most with your audience while also remaining agile enough to pivot your strategies as new data emerges.

Furthermore, actively engage your team members, collaborators, and partners in this process to bring diverse perspectives to the table. This will make it easy to conduct brainstorming sessions and discover innovative solutions that might not have been considered otherwise. Collaboration nurtures creativity, which enables you to develop compelling headlines that not only capture attention but also engage the right people with your content.

An A/B Testing Culture

Create a culture around A/B testing within your organization and encourage team members to suggest ideas and participate in testing initiatives. This collective approach enriches idea generation and builds a robust framework for systematic headline optimization. As various team members propose concepts based on their unique experiences and insights, the pool of potential headline styles grows richer and more varied.

Ultimately, the goal is to establish a dynamic environment where headline crafting becomes a cycle of exploration, testing, and refinement. Be willing to experiment with different types of headlines, such as questions, lists, and statements, while utilizing A/B testing to measure their efficacy (Grigat, 2022). Next, analyze response data diligently to make adjustments and commit to continuous improvement. That's how you'll master the art of writing compelling headlines that capture your audience's attention and drive meaningful engagement.

Learn Secrets of Hooking Headlines

Employing advanced techniques can dramatically elevate the effectiveness of your content when crafting impactful headlines. These include intriguing questions and emotionally charged words that can create an immediate connection with your audience.

Use of Numbers and Lists

Did you know that using numbers and lists is a clever way to gain attention? Numbers create specificity and manage expectations by quantifying what readers will gain from an article. For instance, a headline like "5 Ways to Boost Your Sales Today" clearly signals the reader that they will receive five actionable insights, making it more likely for them to engage. This method also contributes to skimmability, allowing readers to quickly digest the main points of your content (King, 2019).

Captivating Adjectives

Powerful adjectives can evoke emotion, paint vivid images, and spark curiosity. Adjectives such as "unbelievable," "essential," or "transformative" can make your headlines more alluring and relatable. However, it's vital to choose adjectives that genuinely reflect the content and avoid over-exaggeration, as promises exceeding delivery can lead to reader disappointment and reduced trust.

Alliteration and Rhyme

Phonetic techniques like alliteration and rhyme also play a significant role in crafting memorable and catchy headlines. Alliteration can make a headline roll off the tongue, enhancing recall while adding a layer of enjoyment to the reading experience. For instance, "Fantastic Financial Forecasts: Fueling Future Fortunes" employs alliteration to catch the eye and stick in the mind. As Maia Weinstock suggests, alliteration triggers a subtle, pleasing reaction similar to a pun's effect on the human brain, making people feel positively toward your content (Tiên Nguyễn, 2014). Combined with rhyme, these phonetic elements transform a simple headline into something poetic and engaging, encouraging clicks and shares.

Inventing New Words or Phrases

Another technique for headline creation is inventing new words or phrases. This approach sets apart your content by offering something fresh and unique. Creating a buzzword or a quirky phrase can highlight your content's novel aspect, sparking curiosity and discussion. For example, blending ideas into a catchy portmanteau or coining a term relevant to your subject can intrigue audiences. When done thoughtfully, these innovative phrases can become part of the larger conversation, lending recognition and authority to your work.

To create hooking headlines, make sure to follow these guidelines:

- Start the ideation process by brainstorming relevant numbers and items that resonate with your content's core message.

- Identify strong adjectives that accurately convey the significance of your work.

- Play with alliteration and rhythm to create a headline that is informative and engaging.

- Embrace creativity by inventing unique terms or phrases that capture attention.

These techniques require thoughtful application and should always align with your audience's preferences and expectations. A headline needs to be as honest and reflective of the article as possible, aiming not just for clicks but for satisfied retention of the readers who arrive at your content. Remember that engaging headlines bridge the creator and consumer, inviting readers to explore further.

Analyze Successful Headline Case Studies

One of the most effective ways to learn about crafting compelling headlines is by diving into real-world examples that have captured audience attention and driven engagement. Let's explore some insightful case studies, compare headline transformations, recognize success patterns, and consider best practices for crafting headlines.

In-Depth Case Studies

Consider a marketing campaign by a well-known fashion retailer using a headline like "How This Brand Boosted Sales by 50% With a Simple Styling Tip." This headline doesn't just state a fact but creates curiosity and promises valuable insight. The key components here are specific metrics ("boosted sales by 50%") and a concrete benefit ("simple styling tip"). Highlighting practical outcomes tempts readers to uncover the secrets within.

Another excellent example comes from the tech industry: "Revamping Customer Experience: How One Tech Giant Reduced Support Calls by 30%." This brings forward the theme of customer satisfaction, a universally relatable topic, paired with a quantitative achievement. Case studies like these illustrate how numbers not only enhance credibility but also make readers pause and consider what they can learn.

Comparing Before and After

When comparing before and after revisions, it becomes apparent that slight modifications can significantly impact effectiveness. Imagine transforming a vague headline like "Improve Your Marketing Strategy" into something more dynamic like "Triple Your Leads With These Proven Marketing Techniques." The latter is not only specific but also promises actionable results, enticing readers to discover how this tripling feat can be achieved. Such comparisons reveal how specificity and clear benefits often outperform general statements.

Identifying Patterns in Successful Headlines

Through analysis, a recurring trend is the use of direct language and concrete benefits. For instance, the incorporation of phrases like "How to," "Why You Should," or "The Secret to" frequently precedes information that offers immediate value. Headlines that evoke emotion or convey urgency, such as "Unlock the Power of Passion-Driven Marketing Today," attract readers looking for inspiration or quick solutions. Furthermore, acknowledging trends such as the ideal headline length—often cited as around 11 words or 65 characters—can improve readability and engagement. Short enough to maintain attention yet long enough to provide essential details, this balance aids in crafting optimal headlines.

Emulating Best Practices

Replicating best practices from successful headlines involves testing new ideas based on their successes. So, conduct A/B tests where possible: Launch two versions of a headline, gather data on which one performs better, and understand why. For instance, if "10 Ways to Enhance Productivity Now" garners more clicks than "Enhance Productivity With These Tips," it indicates a preference for list-based formats that promise multiple takeaways.

Learning from these tests should guide future attempts. Try integrating emotional triggers or power words like "uncover," "transformation," or "breakthrough," which resonate strongly with audiences seeking change and improvement. Also, consider maintaining clarity over cleverness by ensuring that headline content remains accessible and meaningful.

While emulating successful strategies, ensure you stay updated with changing trends and audience preferences. What worked five years ago might not hold the same allure today due to evolving social dynamics and the rapid pace of digital consumption.

Finally, while experimenting with headlines, remember that consistency across messaging channels enhances brand reputation and recognition. Ensure each headline aligns with your overall branding tone and strategy, reinforcing trust and expectation for reliable content delivery. By doing so, you're not just creating headlines; you're building a narrative your audience depends upon.

Optimize Headlines for SEO

When crafting headlines that capture attention, integrating effective SEO (search engine optimization) practices becomes crucial for attracting organic traffic. Relevant keywords help your audience find you online, but that's not enough. It's also significant to optimize your headlines so they capture attention and signal the value of your content. Ultimately, combining SEO-driven keywords with powerful headlines is the key to increasing the visibility of your content and gaining traffic and engagement to your website.

Finding the Right Keywords

Keyword research is essential for ensuring your content is discoverable by search engines. This involves identifying terms that potential readers will likely use when searching for your topics. High-value keywords not only draw traffic but also align with business goals, such as conversions or brand awareness. Utilize tools like SEMrush or Ahrefs to investigate competitor keywords and identify lucrative opportunities. Focus on long-tail keywords for niche audiences with high intent, as they are often easier to rank for despite lower search volumes. Regularly update your keyword list to align with changing algorithms and user behaviors (Johnson, 2024).

Balancing SEO With Engagement

While it is vital to use keywords strategically, the ultimate goal is to captivate your audience. Your headlines should provoke curiosity and resonate emotionally with readers. Achieving this balance requires creativity—crafting headlines that prioritize readability and clarity. Keywords should naturally fit within the context, avoiding any semblance of stuffing, which can dissuade readers and negatively affect SEO. Search engine algorithms are increasingly advanced and can detect unnatural usage patterns, impacting rankings. Therefore, write for people first and let search engines follow.

Tags and Meta Descriptions

The use of tags and meta descriptions significantly bolsters overall page performance. Meta titles and descriptions provide search engines with context, aiding in indexing and determining relevance (Hardwick, 2020). Incorporate primary keywords in these elements while maintaining brevity and clarity. In practice, aim to keep meta titles under 60 characters and meta descriptions around 160 characters, embedding keywords responsibly for improved click-through rates. Additionally, structured headlines and proper use of image alt tags increase accessibility and appeal to both users and search engines. The practice of including keywords in headings and the initial 100 words of content further strengthens SEO and user experience (Johnson, 2024).

Monitoring the impact on rankings is critical for adapting and refining your strategies. Regularly track keyword performance using analytics and third-party tools like Google Search Console. Also, analyze metrics such as organic traffic, click-through rate (CTR), and bounce rate. These insights reveal how well your headlines are performing and indicate areas for improvement. A high bounce rate might suggest that headline expectations aren't being met in the content, whereas a low CTR could imply that headlines need more allure. Consistently reviewing these metrics allows you to tweak your approach, ensuring your content remains competitive and relevant in the ever-evolving digital landscape.

Summary and Reflections

In this chapter, we've learned the art of headline creation. It consists of promising a benefit or solving a problem to engage your audience. Indeed, we've explored how benefit-oriented language can highlight the reader's gain and why solving problems through strategic headlines resonates with potential customers seeking solutions. The emphasis on clarity over cleverness ensures that your message gets across effectively, making it easier for readers to connect with and trust your brand.

We've also examined the importance of testing different headline styles to see what best captures your audience's attention. Harnessing tools like A/B testing empower you to refine your approach and discover which headlines lead to higher engagement. By analyzing the data gathered, you can adapt your strategies, ensuring that your headlines are not only eye-catching but also informative and relevant. Consistently follow these techniques to obtain compelling headlines that enhance your campaigns and drive sales.

Chapter 4:

Utilizing Emotional Appeals

At the heart of effective communication lies the ability to connect emotionally with your audience, turning mere words into powerful narratives that resonate deeply and inspire action. Whether through stirring stories or creating a sense of urgency, tapping into emotions transforms your message from simple information into meaningful experiences. The magic of emotional appeal lies in its potential to make audiences feel seen and understood, driving them to engage more deeply than ever before.

This chapter explores how to harness the power of storytelling and urgency to create emotional engagement. You'll also learn to employ the Hero's Journey narrative to create relatable and memorable brand stories that hook your audience's feelings. Next, let's discover the power of emotional resonance, the element that turns a good story into one that stays with people, prompting them to share it. We'll look at the importance of visual imagery and user-generated content as well. This helps craft authentic and vivid stories people can truly connect with. Furthermore, you'll learn how to master emotional psychology thanks to core emotional drivers like fear, happiness, and trust. Lastly, we address techniques for creating urgency—a crucial component that propels readers to immediate action, enhancing both engagement and conversion. So, let's dive in and uncover the secrets to writing not just for the mind but for the heart.

Use Storytelling for Relatability and Memorability

In the world of marketing and content creation, storytelling is not just an optional tool—it's a critical technique that enhances connection and recall. When brands include relatable narratives in their marketing strategies, they tap into their feelings and emotions. The way to bridge the gap between your offer and your customers is through stories. As simple as they might seem, stories create vivid imagery and memorable experiences, making it easier for potential customers to recall and relate to your message long after encountering it. The truth is, in a saturated market where attention spans are fleeting, storytelling is the only way to differentiate yourself from others and win the hearts of your audience.

The Hero's Journey

At the heart of storytelling lies the concept of the Hero's Journey, a narrative arc familiar to many. This framework features a protagonist who embarks on an adventure, faces challenges, and ultimately triumphs. To apply this concept, strive to include relatable characters and events in your brand story. That will hook your audience in the best possible way. This structure isn't just about entertainment; it transforms abstract concepts into tangible experiences, making them more engaging and memorable for your audience (*Creating Stories That Stick*, 2023).

Emotional Resonance

But what makes a story truly resonate? It boils down to emotional resonance—the ability of a story to evoke strong feelings. Stories that touch hearts are remembered and shared and keep the audience's attention for a long time (Thoughtlab, n.d.). Think about the last advertisement that made you feel hopeful or inspired—it likely stuck with you longer than any ordinary product description. Emotional resonance makes these stories vivid in our minds, driving home their messages with lasting impact.

Different emotions serve different purposes: joy might encourage positive associations, while fear could highlight urgency. Tailor your story's message to tap into these emotional triggers, ensuring that your narrative doesn't only inform but also moves your audience. Remember, the goal is to communicate and create a lasting emotional hook that keeps your audience coming back.

Visual Imagery

When marketers use descriptive language, they paint pictures in the minds of their readers. This helps the audience visualize scenarios, deepening their connection with the story. For example, instead of saying, "Our product improves productivity," painting a scene where a user seamlessly breezes through their tasks, much like a superhero defeating villains, creates a scenario audiences can see and feel. Such vivid imagery not only aids comprehension but also taps into emotions, making the narrative more compelling and relatable.

Visual imagery, on the other hand, requires a keen focus on language. Use adjectives and metaphors that transport your audience into the world you're crafting. Consider using sensory details that invite the reader to smell, hear, and feel the story unfolding around them. This multi-sensory approach ensures that your narrative doesn't just describe but engages, transforming words into experiences your audience can live through (Brosch, 2018).

User-Generated Storytelling

In today's digital age, user-generated storytelling has become a powerful tool for building authenticity and trust. People connect with real-life experiences, which is why testimonials and customer stories are potent tools. When a customer shares how a product changed their life, it's not just a story—it's a testament to credibility. These authentic narratives enrich brand storytelling, offering proof that goes beyond mere claims. They transform customers into brand advocates, adding a layer of richness and reality to marketing efforts. Incorporating genuine experiences will boost the audience's trust and enhance your brand's reliability (Oladipo, 2022).

To successfully incorporate user-generated content, creating open channels for customers to share their stories is helpful. Encourage reviews, host contests that invite personal narratives, and spotlight these stories across platforms. These initiatives gather authentic content and signal to potential clients that your brand values authentic voices. Highlight the diversity of these experiences, showcasing how your brand impacts lives in various contexts, thus reinforcing the reliability and broad appeal of your offerings.

Mastering Storytelling in a Nutshell

Integrating these elements—the Hero's Journey, emotional resonance, visual imagery, and user-generated content—forms a holistic approach to storytelling. But how does one effectively implement the Hero's Journey in brand storytelling? Understanding its elements is key: the call to adventure (introducing your product), the ordeal (highlighting consumer pain points), and the return (the benefits and solutions your product offers). By structuring brand messages within this framework, you can foster a deeper level of engagement, encouraging customers to invest emotionally in their narrative.

As attention spans dwindle and competition intensifies, the art of storytelling captivates audiences and inspires action. It elevates marketing efforts from mere transactions to meaningful connections and forges enduring relationships with your audience, laying the groundwork for loyalty and advocacy.

Master Emotional Psychology in Selling

Understanding the principles of emotional psychology is essential for anyone looking to craft persuasive copy that genuinely connects with an audience. Persuasive copy reflects human emotions, such as fear, joy, or nostalgia. Did you know that you can tap into these feelings to invoke a desirable response from your readers? That's the power of emotional psychology in selling. Successful messages are neither monotonous nor mundane. They are appealing and relatable to your target audience.

The Core Emotional Drivers

The key to influencing buying behavior is to use core emotional drivers such as fear, happiness, and trust. By comprehending these drivers, you can tailor your messaging to evoke specific responses from your audiences, ultimately motivating action and enhancing engagement.

Let's start with the most powerful core emotional driver: fear. Fear is a strong motivator in decision-making processes (Goyette, 2019). When leveraged appropriately, it can prompt urgency or caution, encouraging consumers to make swift purchasing decisions to mitigate potential losses or dangers. For instance, a home security company might highlight the risks of not having adequate protection, urging customers to invest in their products to ensure safety and peace of mind. However, balancing fear with reassurance is crucial to maintain credibility and avoid alienating the audience.

Happiness, on the other hand, can inspire positive associations with a brand or product. By evoking feelings of joy, pleasure, or contentment, brands can create lasting, favorable impressions that drive loyalty and repeat purchases. For example, a travel agency showcasing beautiful vacation destinations with smiling families can tap into the desire for happiness, effectively persuading potential customers to plan their next trip with them.

Next, there is trust. Trust plays an essential role in influencing consumer behavior. A brand's ability to establish trust can be the deciding factor in whether a customer chooses one product over another. Trust can be fostered through transparent communication, consistent quality, and reliable customer service (Goyette, 2019). Brands like Patagonia have built strong reputations by consistently aligning their messaging with authentic practices, engendering trust and loyalty among their clientele.

Emotionally Driven Messaging

Emotionally driven messaging is all about choosing the right language to elicit emotions effectively. This can involve both positive appeals that inspire hope and excitement and negative appeals that drive urgency or concern. Positive appeals are often seen in charity campaigns, where hopeful storytelling and imagery encourage donations by illustrating the difference contributions can make. Alternatively, negative appeals are frequently used in healthcare messaging, where highlighting potential health risks without certain products encourages preventive actions.

Emotion as a Differentiator

Using emotion as a differentiator is particularly effective in setting copy apart in a saturated market. Emotional storytelling becomes a unique positioning tool for brands aiming to stand out amid noise. Consider the case of Apple's advertising strategy – their ads often focus on emotional narratives surrounding creativity and innovation rather than just product specifications. This approach not only distinguishes them from competitors but also builds a deep emotional connection with their audience.

Balancing Emotion and Rationality

Combining emotion and rationality in copywriting ensures that messages are both compelling and believable. While emotions can drive initial interest and motivation, incorporating logical reasoning solidifies the decision-making process. This balance can be seen in advertisements for environmentally friendly products, which may initially captivate audiences with the feel-good factor of helping the planet, but follow up with logical arguments about cost savings or efficiency benefits. Balancing emotional appeal with factual information is much more effective in creating persuasive communications that resonate on multiple levels (McCormick, 2024).

Take into account the following guidelines when using emotional psychology :

- **Engage the audience's experiences:** Inviting personal relevance nurtures a deeper connection.

- **Encourage user-generated storytelling:** Ask customers to share success stories, adding authenticity and enriching the brand narrative.

- **Leverage testimonials:** Using real examples strengthens trust and emotional ties regarding product benefits.

- **Recognize core emotional drivers:** Tailor messaging to suit the desired response, like inciting action or fostering loyalty.

- **Use emotion as a strategic differentiator:** Balance emotional appeal with rational elements to craft messages that capture attention and leave a lasting impression.

Create Urgency Effectively

Creating a sense of urgency is a great way to compel readers to take action, thanks to the psychological triggers that prompt immediate decision-making. Using tactics such as time sensitivity and emotional triggers in your messages will make it easier for people to decide, which then leads to more engagement and sales.

Scarcity Tactics

Scarcity tactics play on the psychological principle that people value things more when they perceive them as scarce. For instance, highlighting limited stock or offering time-sensitive deals will urge the consumers to buy since you tap into their innate fear of missing out on an opportunity. Consider phrases like "Only five left at this price!" or "Deal ends tonight!" This approach ignites a mental trigger where potential buyers rush to purchase before the offer expires or the product runs out. When customers perceive scarcity, their desire to possess the product or service increases, prompting quicker decision-making (Pascoe, 2024).

Time Sensitivity

Time sensitivity is another critical element in creating urgency. The language used to promote your offers should reflect immediacy. Words and phrases such as "Limited time offer," "Act now," or "Available until midnight" serve as catalysts for immediate action (McCormick, 2024). Countdown timers are particularly effective because they visually reinforce the urgency. As the seconds tick away, potential customers feel compelled to act faster, fearing they'll lose the opportunity if they hesitate. You might see these timers on e-commerce sites during sales events, highlighting how little time remains to secure a deal. Such visual prompts keep the impending deadline at the forefront of customers' minds, driving timely responses.

Emotional Triggers

Emotional triggers linked to urgency play on fears such as missing out (commonly known as FOMO—fear of missing out). This emotional response, when harnessed correctly, can be incredibly motivating. When you emphasize what audiences stand to lose if they don't act immediately, you intensify their need to respond. For instance, "Join today to avoid future price hikes" or "Limited seats available; secure yours now" evoke an emotional reaction that compels quick action. These messages tap into customers' anxiety about being left out or losing a great deal, pushing them towards making a purchase decision with more urgency and less procrastination (McCormick, 2024).

Clear Calls to Action

Clear calls to action (CTAs) are instrumental when building urgency into your copy. A well-crafted CTA does more than just tell customers what to do next; it motivates swift action by using urgent language. Phrases like "Buy now," "Don't wait," or "Start saving today" highlight the necessity of immediate action. Effective CTAs focus on the psychological momentum created by scarcity and time sensitivity, ensuring the potential customer doesn't lose interest by hesitating. This urgency-driven wording guides your audience smoothly from curiosity to conversion, reinforcing the idea that postponing this decision could result in a missed opportunity (McCormick, 2024).

While building a sense of urgency is crucial, balance is needed to maintain credibility and trust. Overuse or insincere claims of shortage can lead to skepticism among savvy consumers who have learned to recognize false urgencies. Thus, delivering genuine value while applying urgency strategies is essential. Make sure your urgent messages are accurate and relevant to build trust with your audience. After all, consumers appreciate transparency and honesty, even amidst the rush of compelling them to act swiftly.

Integrating urgency in a way that resonates with your target audience requires knowing who they are and what motivates them. Different audiences may react differently to various urgency techniques.

Develop Offers Valued Above Cost

Crafting compelling offers that persuade audiences to convert involves creating value propositions that resonate with the audience while exceeding their perceived cost. A potent value proposition is not merely about listing what your product does; it's about highlighting its unique benefits, making it crucial for improving conversion rates. This concept can often be misunderstood as focusing solely on features rather than benefits. In truth, emphasizing benefits over features can offer a more persuasive argument for why your product or service is worth considering.

Value Proposition Essentials

Value proposition essentials play a central role in communicating these benefits effectively. A strong value proposition clearly articulates what makes you different and better than the competition. It must answer questions such as why someone should buy from you instead of others and what immediate and long-term advantages they will gain. For instance, if you're marketing a new software, explain how it will save the user time or increase their productivity instead of simply describing its features. This shifts the focus from mere functionality to the actual impact on the customer's life, which is a much stronger motivator for purchasing decisions.

Bundling Strategies

Next, bundling strategies are another effective way to enhance perceived value. Offering packages or adding bonuses can make standalone products seem more attractive. People often find bundled offers appealing because they perceive greater value in receiving multiple items together at a discounted price compared to buying each separately (Yan et al., 2014). For instance, a gym could bundle a membership with personal training sessions and nutrition guides. This package not only showcases immediate savings but also conveys a comprehensive approach to fitness that might seem more valuable than a standard membership alone.

Psychological Anchoring

Psychological anchoring employs pricing psychology to significantly influence perception. The idea here is to present an initial high-price or premium product next to a standard offering (Ioffe & Borstch, 2023). This approach creates a reference point in the consumer's mind, making the regular price appear more reasonable or even cheap by comparison. For example, when a high-end coffee maker is displayed alongside a lower-priced model, potential buyers may perceive the latter as a great deal, thus driving purchases based on perceived savings.

Demonstrating ROI

This strategy further bolsters the value of an offer by providing evidence-based arguments for its benefits over time. Here, it's critical to move beyond the initial cost and illustrate how the offering contributes to cost savings, increased revenue, or other measurable benefits down the line. A solar panel company, for instance, might demonstrate ROI (return on investment) by showing how energy savings will offset the purchase and installation costs within a specific timeframe, reinforcing the proposition's value through concrete examples.

In this context, demonstrating ROI can also help address some common objections related to cost. Many consumers hesitate to invest in a new product or service due to uncertainties about its long-term benefits. Presenting clear data or case studies that highlight how previous customers have benefited can alleviate these concerns and build trust with potential buyers. Trust is essential because it reassures prospective customers that they're making a sound financial decision.

To fully leverage these strategies, make sure to keep this in mind:

- Ensure your messaging is direct, straightforward, and tailored to customer requirements.

- Clarity is crucial—your value proposition should be instantly recognizable and easy to grasp, considering that web users typically have fleeting attention spans. Potential customers must understand your offer and its uniqueness within seconds. A vague or overly complex message can lead to missed opportunities for conversion due to ineffective communication.

- A value proposition should be flexible. Various audiences may connect with different facets of your offering, so customizing your propositions for diverse market segments can boost engagement and conversion rates. This strategy necessitates a profound understanding of your target demographics, including their likes, challenges, and expectations. Armed with this insight, you can craft specific messages that resonate with different groups, enhancing the chance of conversion across all segments.

- While urgency and exclusivity can drive quicker decision-making through scarcity tactics, avoid bombarding readers with unnecessary guidelines. Striking a balance between thorough instructions and concise persuasion can keep your audience engaged without inundating them with overwhelming details.

Understand What Drives Emotional Action

Grasping the motivations behind consumer behavior is crucial for crafting persuasive writing that truly touches the emotions of the audience. We will explore the intricate factors that influence these motivations to gain valuable insights into what inspires individuals to make decisions, whether they are purchasing a product or engaging with a brand.

Intrinsic vs. Extrinsic Motivations

Intrinsic motivation stems from internal desires, such as personal satisfaction or a sense of accomplishment. For instance, a person may choose to buy organic food because it aligns with their values of health and sustainability. In contrast, extrinsic motivation is driven by external factors like rewards or social recognition. A consumer might purchase a luxury car not only for its features but also for the status it confers. Highlighting intrinsic motivations can create a sense of authenticity and connection, whereas emphasizing extrinsic motivations can appeal to aspirations for social acceptance or recognition (Bernazzani, 2017).

Emotional Triggers

Next, explore emotional triggers, which are powerful tools in persuasive writing. These triggers can elicit immediate responses by tapping into emotions such as fear, sympathy, or happiness (Goyette, 2019). For instance, an advertisement for home security systems might use fear of intrusion as a trigger, urging swift action to ensure family safety. Using emotional triggers implies integrating them seamlessly into messaging to prompt desired actions without appearing manipulative. For example, storytelling that brings out shared human experiences can naturally evoke empathy and drive engagement. These triggers must align with the overall message and brand values to maintain credibility and trust.

Cognitive Dissonance

Cognitive dissonance occurs when consumers experience discomfort due to conflicting beliefs and behaviors. For example, someone might want to indulge in a dessert but feel guilty about the sugar intake. Effective copywriting can address this by providing reassurance, such as highlighting healthier ingredients or promoting moderation. Messages that alleviate cognitive dissonance enhance trust and support customers in their decisions by aligning products with both rational and emotional aspects of choice (Telci et al., 2011). This reassurance can reduce post-purchase regret and promote positive associations with the brand.

Social Influence

The impact of social influence cannot be understated in today's digital age. Social proof, such as endorsements and reviews, powerfully shapes consumer perceptions and can drive emotional responses. When potential customers see others positively engaging with a product, they are more likely to trust the brand and make similar choices (Lua, 2017). Leveraging communal experiences involves showcasing user testimonials, influencer partnerships, or community-driven content to build credibility. For example, a clothing brand might feature customer photos wearing their collections on social media, creating a sense of belonging and encouraging others to join the trend. The perceived authenticity and relatability of peer recommendations significantly bolster audience engagement and conversion rates.

Summary and Reflections

In this chapter, we explored how to connect with your audience through the art of storytelling, focusing on tapping into emotions and creating urgency. We've seen that combining relatable narratives with emotional resonance turns abstract ideas into memorable experiences that stick in the minds of your audience. We've also discussed the importance of crafting visual imagery that invites readers into a vivid world, making them feel like they're part of the story. Moreover, user-generated content serves as a testament to authenticity, inviting real voices to bolster trust and credibility. Together, these elements form a cohesive strategy for engaging audiences on a deeper level.

As you move forward, remember that storytelling isn't just about recounting events; it's about evoking emotions that encourage action. Make sure to tailor your messaging to the key emotions you want to evoke, whether it's joy, fear, or anything in between. Plus, use urgent language to instill a sense of immediacy and drive actions without overwhelming your audience. Importantly, balance emotion with rationality to ensure your copy remains believable and impactful. Applying the nuances of emotional psychology and a sense of urgency will for sure elevate your communication from mere information to building lasting connections with your readers.

Chapter 5:

Incorporating Social Proof

Social proof, such as testimonials, reviews, and endorsements, acts like a powerful magnet, drawing potential customers toward your brand. They help to build credibility and persuade your audience. If used properly and genuinely, these elements can transform your business and lead to massive success. While creating compelling content, you have to understand how authentic voices offer relatable and trustworthy experiences that can influence purchasing decisions. What makes this fascinating is not only the words of praise but also the authenticity behind them, which resonates deeply with consumers. Engaging readers with real-world examples lends weight to the power of social proof, making them more likely to connect emotionally with your brand.

As we explore this chapter, you'll gain insights into leveraging different types of social proof to enhance your marketing strategy. We'll find out how well-placed testimonials can catch your audience's attention in a digital world where content is abundant and patience is scarce. You will also discover strategies for gathering diverse feedback from satisfied customers to create rich narratives, illustrating the numerous benefits your products or services offer. From strategically placing these endorsements to actively encouraging customers to share their authentic experiences, the chapter provides actionable advice on fostering a community around your brand. Additionally, understanding the importance of maintaining authenticity and addressing negative reviews gracefully will turn challenges into opportunities for deeper engagement.

Include Genuine Testimonials and Reviews

The power of real testimonials and reviews cannot be overstated when it comes to building trust and forging connections with potential customers, as they serve as social proof that validates the value of your products or services. When prospective buyers see positive feedback from others who have previously engaged with your brand, they are more likely to feel reassured about their decision-making process and see real value in what you offer. Ultimately, you can leverage these testimonials to enhance your credibility and build your tribe of loyal customers who can also advocate for your brand, encouraging new customers to try your products and become part of your community.

Authenticity Matters

In the increasingly digital market landscape, authenticity plays an essential role in consumer decision-making since genuine testimonials resonate more with audiences than staged or fabricated ones, creating stronger bonds between your brand and its potential buyers. This connection not only leads to higher trust but also increases conversion rates.

When testimonials reflect actual customer experiences, they provide an emotional appeal that scripted reviews simply cannot match (Lua, 2017). This authenticity helps potential clients envision similar successes with your product or service, effectively nudging them toward making a purchase. The strength of honest feedback lies in its ability to make consumers feel secure in their buying decisions, as they're influenced by relatable stories and outcomes.

Diverse Feedback

Collecting testimonials from a variety of customers showcases the wide range of benefits your product or service offers. It illustrates how different audience segments can relate to shared experiences, allowing potential customers to see themselves in the narratives presented. A single glowing review might catch someone's eye, but a collection of diverse testimonials speaks volumes about a product's overall quality and reliability (Lua, 2017). This variety demonstrates that your product meets several needs and preferences, assuring diverse customer bases of its efficacy.

Strategic Placement

Strategic placement of testimonials is key to maximizing their impact. Not every visitor will read through an entire webpage or marketing material word-for-word. By placing testimonials where they're likely to capture attention—such as near-related offerings or call-to-action points—you ensure that skimming readers will still encounter compelling social proof. Visual formats like stylized quotes or video testimonials can further grab users' attention, adding an engaging element that breaks up text-heavy content and maintains viewer interest.

Call to Share

In addition to strategic placement, actively encouraging customers to share their reviews adds significant weight to your social proof strategy. When you prompt customers to leave feedback, you gather valuable insights and help build a community around your brand. Knowing their opinions matters and strengthens customer loyalty and engagement. Besides, offering incentives for reviews, such as discounts or entries into prize drawings, could motivate customers to share their experiences, thereby enriching your collection of testimonials. This sense of involvement strengthens the relationship between your brand and its customers, transforming them from mere purchasers to active participants in the brand's narrative.

To effectively leverage genuine testimonials and reviews:

- Avoid any attempt to manipulate or exaggerate the content of reviews, as authenticity is the foundation of trust (Bishop, 2024).

- Encourage feedback through personalized communication channels preferred by your customers, whether it's email, social media, or direct website interactions.

- Creating a feedback-rich environment where customers feel heard and valued can turn neutral brand experiences into positive testimonials. Exceptional customer service often inspires customers to share their satisfaction publicly.

- Respond promptly and respectfully to both negative and positive reviews. Addressing concerns shows your commitment to customer satisfaction, while acknowledging positive feedback reinforces the value others find in your products or services (Testimonial Donut, 2024).

- Furthermore, incorporating these authentic testimonials seamlessly into your marketing campaigns is a great way to attract potential customers.

- Alongside written stories, video testimonials can remarkably boost emotional engagement. They offer a more personal glimpse at how customers interact with your brand's products or services. These videos can be especially persuasive, bringing words to life and creating a memorable impression on viewers.

Showcase Case Studies for Evidence

Incorporating real-world applications and results into your marketing strategy can serve as incredibly persuasive social proof. You can highlight user success stories, measurable outcomes, relatable challenges, and clear calls to action within case studies to build a bridge of trust between yourself and potential customers.

User Success Stories

User success stories are a powerful testament to the effectiveness of a product or service. They provide narratives that reflect the transformational journey of existing customers, showcasing significant changes they experienced after engaging with a company's offerings. For instance, take the story of an online retailer struggling with declining sales. By using a particular e-commerce platform, they were able to streamline their operations, improve customer satisfaction, and ultimately increase their revenues by 30% within a quarter. Sharing such comprehensive stories highlights the capabilities of the product and inspires confidence among potential buyers who may be facing similar issues. These narratives act like mirrors reflecting prospects' potential futures—successful and improved if they choose to follow suit (Kucukural, 2023).

Measurable Outcomes

Combining these stories with measurable outcomes further adds to their credibility. Quantifiable data can attract the attention of analytical-minded customers, providing them with the assurance they need. Hard data offers a factual backbone to anecdotal evidence, making claims more believable. For example, imagine a tech company that implements its software solution, leading to a 50% reduction in processing time for tasks. Displaying this outcome through graphs or infographics tells a visually compelling story while simultaneously substantiating it with numbers. This approach not only persuades skeptical customers but also enhances the perceived reliability of the information presented. Also, potential customers feel more grounded when they understand the tangible benefits they could receive, transforming initial hesitations into decisive buying actions.

Relatable Challenges

Beyond success stories and tangible results, addressing relatable challenges is critical in resonating emotionally with prospects. When a business articulates the initial hurdles its customers face, whether it's operational inefficiency or resource wastage, it paints a picture that many can relate to. A typical scenario could involve a small business owner struggling to manage multiple aspects of their enterprise single-handedly. When positioning the product or service as a practical, easy-to-adopt solution to these everyday struggles, companies can build an emotional connection with prospects. This helps establish the product as an indispensable tool designed to ease specific pain points rather than just another market offering.

Calls to Action in Case Studies

Lastly, integrating strong calls to action (CTAs) within case studies reinforces the narrative while guiding readers toward taking tangible steps. A robust CTA is useful to align with the success showcased, urging interested individuals to commit to the next step. For example, presenting a compelling case study that outlines how a company doubled its workforce production efficiency could conclude with a call inviting readers to "Request a Demo Today" or "Consult With Our Experts for Tailored Solutions." This ensures that the energy and interest generated throughout the case study do not dissipate, instead channeling it into actionable pathways. Effective CTAs can drive conversions by pushing users from passive reading to active engagement, closing the gap between interest and decision-making.

Use Industry Expert Backing

Industry Validation

Endorsements from industry experts are a game-changer in establishing authority and credibility for products or services. When you associate your brand or products with recognized figures, you can leverage the widespread trust and expertise these individuals command (Vahid Bakhtvar & Piri, 2021). When a reputable expert endorses a product, it signals quality and trustworthiness to potential customers. This endorsement acts as a bridge, connecting the brand's claims with tangible validation from reputable sources. For instance, if a software company seeks to penetrate a highly competitive market, having an endorsement from a renowned tech analyst can significantly bolster the company's reputation. The analyst's positive review not only validates the product's capabilities but also assures consumers of its value.

Content Collaboration

Beyond direct endorsements, content collaboration with industry experts can further enhance credibility while enriching marketing efforts. Collaborations such as webinars, podcasts, or joint articles create a platform for in-depth discussions, offering valuable insights and diverse perspectives. These collaborations enhance the quality of content and engage both the experts and the brand's audiences, expanding the reach and increasing engagement.

To seamlessly integrate expert contributions into content, begin by identifying experts whose work aligns with your brand values and goals. Engage them in conversations about potential topics that resonate with both your target audience and their expertise. Don't forget to provide platforms for these experts to share their knowledge, whether through guest blogging or co-hosting events, to embrace the educational aspect of your content while strengthening relationships with your audience.

Testimonials From Experts

Testimonials from experts serve as reassuring tools to potential customers about the quality and efficiency of a product or service. Unlike generic testimonials, those from recognized experts carry more weight because they come from individuals with significant knowledge and experience in their respective fields. For instance, when a skincare company features testimonials from dermatologists regarding the efficacy of its products, it reassures consumers who might be hesitant due to concerns about skin sensitivity or effectiveness. Expert testimonials provide that extra nudge needed to sway potential customers who value informed opinions.

Promoting Expert Insights

You can condense expert insights into digestible formats to ensure that valuable information is easily accessible to a broad audience. This approach not only aids understanding but also complements storytelling efforts, making the content more engaging and relatable. For instance, summarizing a lengthy expert interview into key takeaways or bite-sized social media posts makes the information quick to consume and easy to share, thereby expanding its reach. This strategy helps build trust by continuously demonstrating a commitment to offering reliable and expert-backed content. Users who see consistent, expert-driven information are more likely to perceive the brand as knowledgeable and trustworthy, ultimately fostering more robust customer relationships (Agnew, 2024).

Incorporating these strategies into marketing campaigns requires attention to detail and execution:

- First, ensure that every piece of expert-driven content is authentic and maintains the expert's voice and perspective. Misquotations or out-of-context snippets can harm credibility rather than build it.

- Use every opportunity to cross-promote expert collaborations, whether through email newsletters, social media, or even traditional advertising channels. Highlighting the partnership with experts in various promotional materials emphasizes the brand's commitment to quality and expertise.

- Additionally, maintaining a relationship with the experts involved is significant for ongoing success. To keep content fresh and relevant, regularly seek their feedback and involve them in future planning.

- Cultivating long-term relationships with experts fortifies trust with audiences and opens doors for future collaborations that can further elevate a brand's standing as a thought leader in its field.

Leverage Data and Statistics as Proof

Incorporating hard data and statistics in your copywriting helps to solidify claims and boost credibility. When audiences encounter data-backed assertions, they are naturally inclined to trust the information presented over mere subjective claims. This is because numbers and facts appeal to logic and reason, offering tangible proof that resonates strongly with a skeptical audience.

Establishing Trust

Let's start by discussing how data establishes trust. Imagine you're presented with two statements: "Our product is popular among users" versus "According to our recent survey, 85% of users reported satisfaction with our product." The latter carries more weight because it supports the claim with concrete evidence. Audiences generally prefer statements fortified by solid data, as this reinforces the authenticity of what's being communicated. In essence, incorporating statistics into your narrative acts like a seal of approval, assuring potential customers that they're making an informed choice grounded in reality (Hicks, 2020).

Visual Representation

Beyond just stating numbers, visually representing data can greatly magnify its impact. Infographics and charts transform complex data into easily digestible visuals, making it simpler for the audience to grasp key messages at a glance. This graphical approach not only aids understanding but also increases engagement. Infographics, in particular, have a high shareability factor, which further amplifies your message's reach. It's beneficial to visually highlight critical statistics to capture the attention of readers who might otherwise skim through text-heavy content. To do so, consider adding clear, engaging visuals to draw readers in and keep them interested, thereby enhancing the overall power of your copy.

Tracking Trends

Another significant advantage of using up-to-date data is tracking trends. Current statistics ensure relevance, signaling to your audience that your brand is aligned with today's market dynamics. Staying relevant in the fast-paced business world is crucial for maintaining authority. To position your brand as forward-thinking and adaptable, why don't you showcase an understanding of ongoing trends? For instance, referencing a recent uptick in eco-friendly purchasing behaviors can highlight your company's commitment to sustainability, further bolstering your credibility. Aligning your messaging with existing trends showcases your proactive approach, which can be particularly appealing to modern consumers looking for brands that understand their evolving needs.

Consumer Behavior Insights

Including research findings in your copy helps validate your value propositions. Data derived from consumer studies sheds light on how your products or services align with current market demands. For example, if research indicates that an increasing number of consumers value digital privacy features, mentioning that your software includes enhanced security measures becomes a compelling argument. Providing such insights empowers prospects to make informed decisions by clearly illustrating how your offerings meet their needs. When prospective buyers see well-articulated, data-supported reasons for choosing your product, they are more likely to move closer to conversion (Hicks, 2020).

To leverage these strategies effectively, it's important to integrate them seamlessly into your writing:

- Clarity and accuracy should always be your top priorities when presenting data. Misrepresenting statistics or presenting them without context can harm your credibility rather than enhance it.

- Always ensure that your data sources are trustworthy and relevant to your claims. Additionally, when possible, provide direct links to sources to allow readers to verify the information themselves—this transparency further bolsters trust.

- While integrating statistics, maintain a conversational tone that keeps your message relatable and engaging. Avoid drowning the reader in numbers; instead, focus on storytelling that weaves data naturally into the narrative.

- For visual representation, remember that simplicity and clarity are key. Design infographics that straightforwardly highlight the most pertinent data, using colors and styles that reflect your brand's identity. Keep in mind that overly complex graphics can detract from comprehension, so prioritize minimalism and readability. Always test the effectiveness of your visuals by considering whether they convey the intended message without additional explanation.

Summary and Reflections

In this chapter, we've explored the transformative power of leveraging testimonials, reviews, and endorsements in your copywriting. Real testimonials do more than simply validate your product; they provide emotional resonance that staged or inorganic reviews simply can't match. Furthermore, addressing a diverse audience through various customer narratives amplifies this effect, painting a holistic picture of how your product or service meets different needs.

Encouraging your customers to share their feedback enhances the richness of your social proof and fosters a sense of community around your brand. Incentivizing reviews aids in gathering a wealth of authentic opinions, nurturing an environment where customers feel valued and heard. This strategy bolsters loyalty, turning casual buyers into active members of your brand story. Additionally, expert endorsements lend an authoritative voice, reinforcing credibility with potential clients who seek knowledgeable validations.

Chapter 6:

Focusing on Benefits

Over Features

Highlighting benefits over features is the secret to communicating value to customers. When you focus on how a product improves life rather than only its technical aspects, you tell a story that resonates more deeply with potential buyers. This approach not only captures attention but also engages emotions, making your message memorable and compelling. As customers become increasingly inundated with choices in the marketplace, understanding this shift will make your offer stand out from the others.

In this chapter, we'll explore the fundamental differences between features and benefits, guiding you to master the art of benefit-oriented messaging. You'll learn how to craft narratives that connect a product's advantages to your audience's daily experiences and aspirations. We will delve into real-world examples that illustrate successful marketing strategies focusing on benefits, providing insights into how leading brands have effectively communicated value.

Translate Features Into Customer Benefits

Focusing on benefits rather than features can transform your copy from generic information into a compelling message. Why? Because the best way to create engaging copy isn't about listing features of your products or services. Instead, it's about focusing on the real value that you can offer to consumers. The key here is to shift the narrative from simply listing what your offer can do to effectively illustrating how it enriches the consumer's life, making solutions tangible and relatable. It means that you can tap into your audience's emotions and desires by answering the critical question that every potential buyer has: "What's in it for me?" and you can do so through your copy. Let me tell you how.

Understanding the Feature-Benefit Relationship

The relationship between features and benefits is a critical aspect of any marketing strategy. While features describe a product's technical or physical characteristics, benefits highlight the personal gain or satisfaction a consumer derives from those features (Copywriting.org, 2023b). This is why understanding this relationship is so vital, as it helps clarify why customers should care about the product. For example, consider an advanced smartphone with a high-quality camera—this feature matters less on its own but becomes highly relevant when translating into the benefit of capturing professional-grade photos effortlessly.

Benefit-oriented messaging appeals directly to customer needs, effectively increasing engagement. Focusing on how a product meets specific desires or solves the issues of your target audience is the best way to create a more compelling narrative. It's not just about what the product does but about the positive change it brings to a user's life.

Case Studies and Examples

Let's consider the marketing strategies of companies like Apple and Nike. Apple doesn't just advertise the specs of its products; it emphasizes how each device simplifies and enriches users' lives through seamless integration and aesthetic design, thus painting a picture of a lifestyle enhanced by technology. Similarly, Nike focuses not only on the technical aspects of its gear but also on the empowerment and performance improvement athletes experience using their products. These narratives go beyond mere functionality, resonating deeply with audiences and driving purchasing decisions.

Guidelines for Using Benefit-Oriented Messages

To translate features into benefits, make sure to keep the following key points in mind:

- Practice creating benefit-driven messages to reinforce your understanding and boost your persuasive writing confidence.

- Engage in exercises that transform standard product features into impactful benefit statements. For example, instead of just stating "extended battery life," articulate it as: "With extended battery life, you can effortlessly connect and cherish moments throughout the day."

- Recognize that the choice of words can significantly shape audience perceptions. During practice, evaluate how different phrasing can alter how a product is viewed.

- Simplify your language when transitioning to a benefit-oriented approach. Stay away from technical jargon or convoluted explanations that might alienate potential readers. Use clear, relatable language to ensure your message resonates with a broad audience.

- Leverage simple storytelling techniques to effectively illustrate the value of benefits, often finding that clear narratives convey importance better than complex feature descriptions.

- Establish emotional connections by aligning product benefits with familiar experiences. To do so, harness the power of emotional appeal, which taps into the feelings and aspirations of your audience, promoting actions that resonate with them (Carmicheal, 2021).

- Begin by identifying your product's primary benefits and crafting a narrative centered around these advantages. Involve your audience by gathering feedback or conducting surveys to determine which benefits resonate best with them for maximum relevance and impact.

- Ensure that every communication channel reflects a unified benefits-driven message. Consistency across social media, email campaigns, and website content enhances credibility and increases customer conversion opportunities.

Articulate Clear Value Propositions

A value proposition must capture customer attention while differentiating one's product or service from competitors. It is not merely a tagline or catchphrase; it's a comprehensive statement that expresses why a consumer should choose your offering over others. Consider it an elevator pitch for your brand—succinct yet impactful.

Components of an Effective Value Proposition

To define a compelling value proposition, focus on three core elements: clarity, benefits, and distinctiveness. Clarity involves articulating your message in straightforward terms, avoiding industry jargon that could alienate those unfamiliar with the field. The goal is to tell your audience exactly what you're offering without ambiguity. For example, instead of saying, "Our software optimizes processes," specify how it saves time or reduces errors.

Next, emphasize benefits rather than features. While features describe what a product can do, benefits tell the customer how it will improve their life or business. This shift appeals directly to customer needs and helps forge a connection based on value. For instance, highlighting how a feature like cloud storage ensures secure data access anywhere can resonate more than simply stating its availability.

Distinctiveness encompasses what makes your offer unique. It's about identifying your unique selling point (USP) and communicating this effectively. Whether it's innovative technology, exceptional service, or unmatched expertise, your USP should assure customers they are making the best choice by opting for your solution.

Creating Value Propositions

One practical method for crafting a persuasive value proposition is brainstorming, followed by iterative refinement. Begin by gathering a diverse team to brainstorm ideas about your product's unique benefits and customer needs. Encourage creativity and openness, allowing everyone to contribute thoughts and experiences. Capture all ideas initially, then refine them by assessing each one's clarity, relevance, and distinctiveness.

Once you've narrowed down your propositions, test them using feedback from current customers and stakeholders. Online A/B testing can also give insights into which messaging resonates most effectively. Remember, your value proposition isn't set in stone—it should evolve based on customer preferences and market dynamics.

Let's consider an example that illustrates compelling value propositions in action. Imagine a subscription box company that delivers gourmet snacks. Instead of focusing solely on the variety and international origins of the snacks (features), the company highlights how these curated selections bring joy and surprise to everyday moments (benefits). By doing so, they tap into the emotional element of curiosity and delight, which enhances customer satisfaction and loyalty.

Such examples demonstrate how businesses across various industries translate features into compelling benefits that emphasize their value. Studying these models helps distill lessons from effective copywriters and marketers, enriching your strategy with proven tactics.

Use Relatable Benefit Statements

Crafting a connection with your audience through benefit-focused and relatable language is all about aligning communication with everyday experiences familiar to your audience. When you craft language that reflects their daily lives, you create a bridge between what you're offering and what they need or desire, making your message more impactful and persuasive.

Finding Common Ground

Actively listening to your audience's feedback helps find common ground, which gives you invaluable insights into their preferences, challenges, and aspirations. This information allows you to tailor your messaging to reflect their concerns and experiences, creating a sense of understanding and community. Interviews, whether conducted online or face-to-face, provide richer, qualitative data that can reveal motivations and emotional triggers. These personal touchpoints ensure that the language used resonates on an individual level, making the message feel less like a sales pitch and more like a conversation between friends.

Personal interactions not only yield deeper insights but also create meaningful connections, transforming your messaging from mere transactional language into relatable conversations. This shift in approach enhances engagement, encouraging customers to share their own experiences and fostering a loyal community around your brand. And when your audience perceives that you are genuinely attuned to their needs, they are more likely to trust your brand and remain loyal to it.

Effective Benefit Statements

Benefit statements are the ticket to winning the hearts of your audience. While features tell what a product does, benefits explain why it matters and how it positively affects the customer's life. For instance, instead of stating that a smartphone has an advanced camera, highlight how it allows users to capture precious memories with stunning clarity, enhancing their ability to relive cherished moments. If you weave emotional appeal with practical advantages, you demonstrate value and invoke feelings of desire and necessity, driving deeper engagement and connection. It's about painting a picture where customers see themselves enjoying the benefits seamlessly integrated into their lives.

The following guidelines will help you take product features and create narrative-driven statements that highlight customer benefits:

- Role-playing activities enable you to step into the shoes of various personas within your target audience, allowing you to explore unique perspectives and emotional reactions.

- It's essential for you to tackle common hurdles in differentiating benefits from features.

- As you gain confidence in delivering persuasive messages, your capacity to connect with audiences on an emotional level flourishes.

- This enhancement fosters greater customer loyalty and boosts conversion rates, creating wins for both you and the business.

Avoid Jargon; Clarify Feasible Advantages

The words you choose can either hook your customers or push them away. Hence, clarity is key; the more straightforward and relatable your language, the more likely it is that they will grasp the value of your offer and see how it meets their needs. And that should be the primary aim of your copy. If they understand what you're trying to convey, they'll likely get more interested and engaged in what you're offering. Therefore, it's imperative to prioritize clear and accessible language over jargon and complex terms. Let's elaborate on this method a little further.

Jargon and Its Pitfalls

One of the main hurdles of communication is the use of jargon. Jargon implies specialized terms that may be familiar to experts and industry insiders but alienate ordinary customers. These terms can create a barrier between you and your audience, making it difficult for the latter to understand the essential messages being conveyed. When people encounter jargon, they often feel excluded, leading to a sense of frustration or even distrust. This feeling of being on the outside can hinder a customer's willingness to engage or transact.

Imagine walking into a store where everyone spoke a language you didn't understand; you'd likely feel lost and confused, ultimately walking out without making a purchase. In the same vein, when customers are bombarded with technical language or industry-specific terminology, they may disengage from the conversation altogether. The same holds for customer interactions: clear communication that avoids the pitfalls of jargon encourages an environment of openness and trust. Hence, using plain language that resonates with your audience is highly beneficial if you want to bridge the gap between your offer and your audience. In the end, this will ensure meaningful dialogue and interaction, which increases the chance of you making sales and gaining trust from customers.

Simplicity Over Complexity

To create clear messaging that resonates with your audience, it's important to simplify your language. This doesn't mean dumbing down your content; the goal is to make it understandable to everyone, regardless of their background (Ashley, 2024). One effective method is to conduct readability tests. These tests analyze your text to determine its complexity level, offering suggestions on how to make it more readable. Tools like Flesch-Kincaid readability tests evaluate sentence length and word difficulty, guiding you toward simpler phrasing.

Another useful technique is peer review. Having others—especially those who represent your target audience—review your content can provide invaluable insights into how understandable and appealing it is. Feedback from peers can highlight areas lacking clarity and suggest alternatives that might better convey your intended message.

How Clear Language Makes Your Product a Winner

Before-and-after examples are powerful tools for demonstrating the impact of eliminating jargon. Consider a tech company's product description. The original version, laden with technical terminology, might read: "Utilizing a quadrilateral processing system with hyper-threading capabilities." For the average consumer, this doesn't convey much. A simplified version could say: "Faster performance for seamless multitasking." The latter paints a clear picture of the benefits—speed and efficiency—making it more relatable and appealing to potential buyers.

The clarity offered through plain language extends beyond ease of understanding; it significantly impacts customer preference (Ashley, 2024). Customers appreciate straightforward communication because it respects their time and intelligence. When people quickly grasp what a product or service can do for them, they're more inclined to engage with the brand. In turn, this approach cultivates trust, as transparency suggests honesty and reliability.

Emphasizing Feasible Advantages

In addition to simplifying language, highlighting a product's feasible advantages can solidify customer trust. This involves presenting benefits in a compelling manner that resonates emotionally and logically with your audience. For example, instead of merely stating that a car has high fuel efficiency, emphasize the benefits: "Save money every month and reduce your environmental footprint with our eco-friendly design." Such statements connect with customers' values and priorities, reinforcing that the company understands their needs and cares about delivering genuine value.

Ultimately, focusing on benefits rather than features requires a shift in perspective. It involves looking through the eyes of the customer and addressing their pain points directly (Carmicheal, 2021). When crafting your message, always ask yourself: *How does this benefit the customer? What problem does it solve in their lives?* This mindset ensures that you're not merely listing attributes but explaining why those attributes matter to the customer.

It's essential to recognize that in today's fast-paced world, customers often skim content before diving into details. Therefore, initial impressions count. Start with the most impactful benefits up front, making immediate connections between the product and the customer's needs. This upfront clarity encourages further exploration, leading customers to delve deeper into what you're offering.

Add Perceived Value to Your Offer

Perceived value goes beyond a product's physical characteristics or features; it focuses on how consumers view and evaluate the benefits that a product or service provides. This perception significantly influences consumer decision-making, dictating whether they will make a purchase or remain loyal to a particular brand. Marketers must comprehend that perceived value doesn't always align with actual value. It's about the consumer's belief in the advantage they'll gain from using your product or service.

Enhancing Perception

One effective way to boost perceived value is by employing techniques such as bundling and leveraging testimonials (WordStream, 2024). Bundling involves packaging several products or services together at a reduced price, which can create the impression of receiving a better deal. This method not only increases sales but also enhances the consumer's perception of the value received. Testimonials, on the other hand, harness social proof. When potential customers see positive feedback or recommendations from others, especially those they consider peers, they are more likely to believe in the product's worth. Incorporating authentic user experiences and success stories into marketing strategies can dramatically raise the perceived value of offerings.

The Power of Branding

Branding is the art of creating a unique identity around a product, service, or company in the minds of consumers. It encompasses a variety of elements, including the name, logo, design, messaging, and overall experience associated with the brand. Branding aims to differentiate yourself in the marketplace, attracting customers and building loyalty and trust. Most importantly, the power of branding lies in its ability to influence the audience's perceptions of your product or service. For example, a well-established brand can translate quality, reliability, safety, a sense of community, and partnership or value.

Branding plays a significant role in shaping perceived value through storytelling and consistency. A strong brand tells a compelling story that resonates with its audience, creating an emotional connection that goes beyond the product itself (AI Contentfy Team, 2023). Consistent branding across all channels ensures that the message stays coherent and reinforces trust among consumers. For example, a luxury brand that consistently portrays exclusivity and superior quality in its narrative and visual identity will maintain a high perceived value. Brands must consciously craft their messages and maintain consistency to reinforce the perceived value over time.

Monitoring Changes to Enhance

Monitoring changes in perceived value can be achieved through collecting feedback, conducting competitive analysis, and performing A/B testing. Feedback allows companies to understand what aspects of their offerings are valued by consumers and what might need improvement. Competitive analysis helps identify strengths and weaknesses in comparison to rivals, providing insights into areas where perceived value can be enhanced. A/B testing different marketing approaches or product offers can reveal what resonates most with your target audience, enabling fine-tuning strategies to maximize perceived value.

Incorporating these principles into marketing strategies is paramount for any business intent on thriving in today's competitive landscape. Using techniques such as bundling and leveraging personal stories or testimonials can increase the perceived value of your offer. Moreover, consistently communicating your brand's story strengthens consumer trust and loyalty, while regular monitoring through feedback and testing ensures that the perceived value remains aligned with evolving consumer preferences.

Final Insights

As you've navigated through this chapter, we've delved into the art of translating product features into customer benefits, a critical strategy for effective marketing communication. The emphasis has been on shifting from a list of technical specs to painting a vivid picture of how these features improve the lives of your customers. While features are important, it's the benefits that resonate with customers and drive their buying decisions. Through compelling narratives and real-world examples, you've seen how brands like Apple and Nike successfully communicate value by aligning their messages with consumer needs and emotions.

Now, the power to craft engaging, benefit-oriented messages lies at your fingertips. You can achieve such a goal by striving to maintain a relatable language and emotional appeal to build connections that go beyond simple transactions, creating trust and loyalty with your audience. Remember to keep the message clear and straightforward, ensuring it speaks directly to what your audience values most. With practice and a keen understanding of your audience's desires, you can enhance your copywriting skills and, in turn, elevate your marketing strategies to new heights.

Chapter 7:

Creating a Strong Call to Action

Crafting a strong call to action (CTA) is central to effective communication with your audience. CTAs are not just closing lines in marketing materials but gateways to meaningful interaction and conversion. Understanding what makes a CTA compelling can significantly influence the decisions of potential customers. The right wording invites an immediate response, guiding people toward actions like making purchases or signing up for newsletters. Captivating CTAs helps eliminate hesitation, making them paramount in navigating readers toward a desired outcome smoothly and effectively.

This chapter elaborates on various strategies for designing CTAs that capture attention and drive engagement. It explores how clarity and directness should be at the heart of every well-crafted CTA, ensuring the message is easily understandable amid today's fast-paced digital environment. You'll learn how visual placement and color contrast play crucial roles, as these factors can dictate a CTA's visibility. You'll also discover the power of action-oriented verbs that evoke a sense of urgency and command attention. The importance of aligning CTAs seamlessly within content is highlighted as a technique to maintain narrative flow and reinforce trust.

Design Clear and Direct CTAs

Creating a compelling call to action (CTA) involves several strategic elements as criteria, such as clarity and directness, should guide potential customers toward taking action. A well-crafted CTA not only clearly articulates what the audience should do next—whether it's "Sign Up Now," "Get Your Free Trial," or "Shop Today"—but also instills a sense of urgency and importance, compelling users to act promptly.

Understanding the psychology behind a CTA can significantly enhance engagement and conversion rates; for instance, employing action-oriented language and appealing to emotions can make the message more relatable and persuasive. Let's break these down.

Simplicity

First and foremost, simplicity is key in crafting a compelling CTA. In a digital age where attention spans are shrinking, your message must be clear and concise. On one hand, a straightforward CTA ensures that readers quickly understand what action they are expected to take, whether it's signing up for a newsletter, downloading a resource, or making a purchase (Stillgoe, 2024). On the other hand, complex language or ambiguous phrasing can easily confuse potential customers, causing them to hesitate or disengage altogether. For example, instead of saying, "Explore our range of innovative solutions," a simple "Discover our products" might be more effective. The latter option directs the reader precisely toward the intended action without causing any ambiguity.

Consistency With Content

Equally important is ensuring that the CTA aligns seamlessly with the surrounding content. A CTA should not feel jarring or out of place; instead, it should follow logically from the information preceding it. This alignment helps maintain a natural flow and guides the reader smoothly toward the desired outcome. If a blog post discusses tips for improving home safety, a CTA inviting readers to download a free home safety checklist would naturally fit and encourage further engagement. This approach not only enhances the coherence of the narrative but also reinforces trust among readers by showing them that their needs and interests have been anticipated (Stillgoe, 2024).

Visibility Matters

Visibility is another critical factor in the effectiveness of CTAs. To stand out and prompt action, CTAs should be positioned prominently within the design layout. Using contrasting colors can significantly enhance their visibility, ensuring they capture attention even during a quick scan of the page. However, choosing the right colors involves more than just bright hues; it requires an understanding of color psychology and how different shades interact on a webpage. For instance, a bright orange button might effectively pop on a dark blue background but could lose its impact on a similarly bright background (Dobre, 2013). Thus, selecting a color palette that complements the overall design while ensuring enough contrast to catch the eye is crucial for drawing attention and enticing action.

Strategic Placement

The placement of a CTA within the content is also significant. Strategic positioning—such as placing CTAs above the fold—can increase visibility and interaction, especially since users often skim rather than thoroughly read content. Placing a CTA in a region where users naturally focus their attention, like the center of the screen, ensures maximum exposure. Moreover, considering different device screens, such as desktops versus mobiles, is essential to ensure CTAs remain visible and effective regardless of the viewing platform (Stillgoe, 2024). Responsive design principles allow adjustments to be made so that CTAs are appropriately sized and positioned for all devices.

Clear and Authoritative Language

In addition to visual strategies, employing strong, authoritative language in CTAs can greatly influence user actions. Commanding words reduce room for interpretation and convey confidence in the offer. Verbs like "Join," "Download," "Start," and "Buy" create a sense of immediacy and instruction, minimizing the cognitive load on the user. Instead of inviting users to "Consider joining our community," a more direct "Join our community today" leaves little doubt about the next step. This authoritative tone reassures users that they are making a positive choice, increasing the likelihood of conversions.

While clarity and directness form the backbone of compelling CTAs, these elements do not exist in isolation. They intersect with other factors like message alignment, color contrast, strategic placement, and language to create a holistic approach to conversion optimization. I suggest you try various combinations of these elements to determine what resonates best with your audience.

Use Action-Oriented Command Verbs

When we consider the power of language in crafting effective calls to action (CTAs), action verbs emerge as pivotal tools that can significantly impact reader motivation and response rates. Action verbs are potent because they convey a sense of immediacy and compel readers to take notice and act. These action-oriented words energize the message, making it more compelling and engaging for the audience. These powerful words can create CTAs that attract attention and encourage swift action. By tapping into the psychology of urgency, action verbs instill a sense of importance and immediacy, encouraging readers to act swiftly rather than procrastinate. This is particularly crucial in a fast-paced digital environment where attention spans are limited and competition for engagement is fierce. The effectiveness of a CTA can often be traced back to the choice of words, and action verbs stand out as the key elements that can drive readers to react decisively.

Active Voice

Active voice paired with command verbs like "Join," "Download," and "Subscribe" infuses energy and urgency into CTAs. These words do more than just instruct—they invite participation. Imagine being on a webpage where you're told to "Download your free guide today." The active voice here doesn't just suggest an action; it creates a sense of necessity and willfulness. This direct approach is key for driving engagement. Inactive language, by contrast, can drain the CTA of its immediacy, making it less compelling and sometimes overlooked.

In contrast, inactive language can drain a CTA, making it less compelling. When language is passive or vague, it can lead to confusion or uncertainty in the reader's mind, diminishing their motivation to engage with the content being offered. Phrases that lack clarity can leave potential participants feeling uninspired or indifferent, ultimately failing to capture their attention. Always pick vibrant and assertive language to ensure your calls to action stand out and, importantly, to grab attention, propel decisions, and reduce procrastination from your readers.

Emotional Connection

Another powerful aspect of action-oriented terms is their ability to tap into emotional connections, providing more substantial incentives for action. Words carry weight, and when chosen carefully, they can resonate deeply with the audience's feelings and desires. Verbs such as "Discover now" or "Unlock secrets" don't just tell people what to do; they promise an experience or transformation, tapping into curiosity and the human desire for improvement (McFarland, 2024). These emotionally charged verbs excite and intrigue, making the prospect of taking action more enticing. Through this emotional appeal, action verbs can bridge the gap between simply clicking a button and feeling motivated to engage with the brand or product idea on offer.

Brevity Is Powerful

Keeping commands short and punchy helps prevent confusion or disinterest among readers. A concise CTA removes any hesitation about what needs to be done and why it matters. For instance, a simple "Shop Now" button is easy to understand and leaves no room for ambiguity. On the other hand, a lengthy CTA will hinder the message and lose its impact. Simplicity ensures clarity, making it easier for the audience to decide quickly without being bogged down by superfluous information. By maintaining brevity, CTAs can effectively capture attention in the fast-paced digital landscape where every second counts.

Consistency in Tone

The choice of verbs must also align with the overall brand tone to maintain consistency and reliability. Consistency in communication reinforces a brand's identity and builds trust with the audience. If a brand's voice is casual and friendly, then CTAs should reflect that persona rather than adopting a formal or harsh approach. For example, a playful brand might use "Get It" instead of "Purchase Now," subtly reinforcing its laid-back image while still driving action. It's essential that the CTA feels like a natural extension of the brand's voice, creating a seamless reading experience that encourages positive engagement and fosters customer loyalty (McFarland, 2024).

It's important to consider the alignment between the choice of words and the brand voice to tailor successful CTAs. This congruence is vital for building a coherent narrative that readers can easily follow and relate to. When CTAs feel out of place or inconsistent with the rest of the content, they risk alienating potential customers or breaking their immersion. Therefore, selecting verbs that resonate with and reinforce the brand's core messages supports long-term success.

Position CTAs Strategically in Copy

The strategic placement of Calls to Action (CTAs) within your content aims to capture and maintain reader engagement. When CTAs are positioned optimally, they become more effective in guiding readers toward taking desired actions, whether it's signing up for a newsletter, downloading an e-book, or making a purchase. Here's where and how to place these prompts to impact visibility and user interaction.

Above the Fold

One of the most effective strategies for CTA placement is positioning them above the fold. This part of your webpage is what users see without needing to scroll, making it prime real estate for important messages. Since a substantial portion of users skim content, having a CTA visible right from the beginning ensures that it catches their eye before they move on. This immediate visibility increases the chance of engagement and sets a direct path for action from the outset, tapping into the initial curiosity or interest that brought the user to your page in the first place (BuzzBoard, 2024).

After Compelling Content

Another key moment for placing CTAs is immediately after engaging content. When readers reach this point, they are typically at peak interest, having just absorbed valuable information or been entertained by what they've read. Capitalizing on this heightened engagement by placing a well-crafted CTA can lead to increased conversions. It acts as a seamless transition from content consumption to action-taking, leveraging the momentum generated by the content itself.

Throughout the Content

For longer pieces of content, strategically inserting CTAs throughout the text helps maintain reader interest and engagement. Long articles or guides can risk losing readers halfway through if there are no hooks to keep them connected. Sprinkling CTAs throughout will guide readers along their journey, reminding them of potential actions without being overly intrusive. This method ensures that even if they don't reach the end of the article, there's still a chance they'll encounter and act on a CTA.

In Conclusion Sections

After delivering comprehensive and engaging content, ending with a robust call to action reinforces the journey you've led the reader on. It serves as a capstone to their experience, leaving them with a definitive next step. A concluding CTA should reflect the entirety of the content's message, urging the reader to act while their interest and the information are fresh in their mind (Dobre, 2013). This final push can prompt them to move beyond consuming content and toward meaningful interaction with your brand or service.

To illustrate, consider the approach of a fitness blog offering a free workout plan. At the top of the post, a CTA invites readers to download the plan. Midway, another CTA highlights success stories from others who used the plan, encouraging sign-ups through social proof. The article concludes with a CTA reiterating the benefits of the workout and nudging readers to start their fitness journey. This strategic layering of CTAs ensures maximum exposure and engagement at various points of reader interaction.

Visibility matters in each of these instances. Using contrasting colors and prominent placement can enhance click-through rates by differentiating CTAs from other elements on the page, making them stand out. If readers can easily find the CTA, its effectiveness naturally increases. Additionally, familiarity with web design elements can aid in better placement, ensuring that CTAs are intuitively positioned where users expect to find them, thereby reducing friction in the decision-making process.

Test CTA Phrasing and Placement

In the dynamic world of crafting calls to action, where even minor tweaks can vastly improve engagement, A/B testing emerges as a crucial tool. Employing A/B testing helps to experiment with various elements of CTAs—such as text, color, and placement on a webpage—to discern what truly resonates with their audience. This method allows for data-driven decisions that enhance the effectiveness of these vital prompts, ultimately leading to increased conversions and engagement.

Experimenting With Variants

To begin experimenting with different texts, colors, and positions of your CTAs, consider creating multiple variants of a single CTA. For instance, one version might use more vibrant colors to catch the eye, while another opts for subtler tones aligned with your brand's aesthetic. Varying the position of the CTA on the page is equally important; a button placed right after an engaging piece of content can capture readers at the height of their interest, prompting immediate action. Through systematic testing, you can collect valuable insights into which combinations attract the most interactions, thereby informing your future design choices.

Analyzing Click-Through Rates (CTR)

CTR serves as a direct indicator of a CTA's effectiveness, reflecting how many users are compelled to take action out of the total who viewed the message (Dobre, 2013). Analyzing these metrics lets you gauge the success of each variant in your A/B tests. For example, if a particular color scheme leads to a noticeable increase in CTR, it suggests that this visual element aligns well with audience preferences. Tracking these changes over time helps build a clearer picture of what drives user interaction, enabling more strategic refinements.

Feedback Loops

Feedback loops play a significant role in refining CTA practices. Audience feedback offers invaluable qualitative data that complements the quantitative insights from CTR analysis. Establishing channels for direct input, such as surveys or user interviews, can reveal why certain CTAs are more appealing than others. This qualitative feedback is the key to understanding the underlying motivations driving user behavior, allowing you to tweak the language and design of CTAs to better align with customer expectations and desires. Implementing these feedback loops ensures that your CTA strategies remain responsive and relevant, adapting swiftly to changing preferences.

Documenting Learnings

Incorporating A/B testing into your CTA development process not only enhances the immediate efficacy of your marketing efforts but also cultivates a deeper understanding of your audience's preferences and behaviors. Keeping detailed records of each A/B test, including the variations tested, results, and any external factors that might have influenced outcomes, creates a valuable resource for future reference. Over time, these documented insights can highlight emerging patterns across different campaigns and audiences. Recognizing such trends enables you to anticipate user responses better and tailor your CTAs accordingly.

Encourage Scarcity and Limited-Time Offers

Scarcity marketing is a strategic approach that capitalizes on this concept by making consumers feel they must act quickly before an opportunity slips away. The psychological trigger of urgency can be incredibly powerful, compelling people to make decisions hastily in fear of missing out on a valuable offer. Let's explore how scarcity and urgency work together to craft CTAs that attract attention and drive conversions.

Urgency Triggers

One of the most effective ways to infuse urgency into your CTAs is through time-sensitive phrases like "Limited Time Offer." These words signal to the consumer that the opportunity will not last, prompting immediate consideration and action. Research suggests that urgency is a time-based motivator that pushes individuals to act swiftly, driven by the fear of missing out (FOMO) (Brebion, 2018). You can harness this psychology to achieve rapid responses from your audience.

Limited Availability

Alongside explicit urgency triggers, clearly stating the limited availability of a product or service amplifies its desirability. When consumers perceive that an item is scarce, they often assume it must be valuable (Brebion, 2018). This perception heightens their interest and makes them more inclined to act while they still can. It taps into the scarcity principle, where the rarity of an object is equated with greater value. When you emphasize how many items are left or how long a deal lasts, you create urgency and enhance the perceived value of your offering.

Promotional Timers

Visual cues can further bolster the sense of urgency in your CTAs. Countdown timers, for instance, serve as a dynamic reminder of the narrowing window of opportunity. They create a visual representation of time slipping away, which can effectively spur consumers into making quicker decisions. Using countdowns in emails or landing pages can dramatically increase engagement rates by visually captivating the viewer and instilling a sense of haste.

Balancing Scarcity and Authenticity

Overusing these different tactics or employing them disingenuously can erode trust and damage brand reputation. Consumers today are savvy and can detect when urgency feels manufactured or manipulative. For example, if a sale is constantly labeled as "limited time" yet reappears frequently, consumers may start to doubt its legitimacy. Maintaining transparency and genuinely limiting offers ensures that urgency marketing does not backfire, preserving customer trust and loyalty over time.

To implement scarcity marketing effectively, consider the following guidelines:

- Use active voice in your CTAs to direct customers confidently.

- Harness the power of engaging language, paired with visuals, to convey urgency and create an emotional connection with the audience.

- Keep your message concise to prevent any confusion and allow the main point—the urgent need to act—to shine through.

In practice, major corporations successfully use scarcity marketing techniques to engage and convert. For example, Amazon's "Today's Deals" section showcases limited-time discounts that naturally stir excitement and prompt immediate purchases. Booking.com similarly displays messages like "Only 2 rooms left!" to urge potential guests to book without hesitation (Edwards, 2024). These examples demonstrate how creating a genuine and transparent sense of urgency can lead to increased customer actions.

When framed authentically, scarcity marketing offers a unique way to communicate value and importance, showcasing a sense of exclusivity among consumers. When clients know that certain deals are not always available to everyone, they might feel special and valued, encouraging repeat business and strengthening brand loyalty.

While crafting CTAs with built-in urgency is undoubtedly effective, you should always monitor responses and be prepared to modify your approach based on feedback. Regularly updating tactics based on consumer reactions ensures that your strategy remains fresh and engaging rather than predictable or repetitive. Transparency and honesty are critical; misleading claims can undermine trust, so your promotions must always match reality to maintain credibility.

Summary and Reflections

In this chapter, we've explored the key elements of creating effective calls to action (CTAs) that genuinely resonate with readers. A compelling CTA is a blend of clarity, strategic placement, and powerful wording. Make sure your CTAs are direct and simple so customers can easily understand what you're asking them to do—whether it's subscribing to a newsletter or making a purchase. Additionally, placing CTAs in logical parts of your content, such as after valuable information or above the fold, maximizes their visibility and potential impact. Using vivid colors and aligning your message with the surrounding content further enhances their effectiveness and helps foster trust among your audience.

As we conclude our discussion on CTAs, remember how action-oriented verbs and concise language can elevate your prompts. These minor adjustments not only capture attention but also encourage quick decisions from your audience. By experimenting with different phrasings and placements through A/B testing, you gain valuable insights into what works best for your audience, allowing you to continuously refine your approach. The power of urgency and scarcity can amplify your CTAs, enticing immediate responses when applied authentically.

Chapter 8:

Practicing Persuasive Techniques

Practicing persuasive techniques comes down to transforming ordinary copy into compelling messages. These techniques aim to capture attention and inspire action through writing. The world of copywriting is not simply about stringing words together; it's an art form that requires skill in crafting and delivering messages that resonate with the audience.

In this chapter, you will learn the various methods of persuasion that serve as the foundation of effective copywriting. You'll explore how to implement strategies like the AIDA model, which guides writers from capturing attention to encouraging decisive action. Besides, understanding the power of specific words and phrases can dramatically enhance the potency of your message, tapping into deep-seated human desires and emotions. Lastly, the principle of reciprocity, along with the magical balance of logic and emotion, can make your writing convincing and relatable. Each section provides practical insights into how these techniques can be woven into your content, ensuring that your copy doesn't just reach its audience but engages and inspires them.

Implement AIDA Formula

In persuasive copywriting, it's important to structure content effectively to guide potential customers through their decision-making process. One tried-and-true method to achieve this is employing the AIDA model, which stands for attention, interest, desire, and action (Sellers, 2022). This model helps guide writers in crafting content that captures a reader's attention, nurtures their interest, builds desire, and ultimately encourages them to take action. Let's dive into how each component of AIDA can be implemented in your copy:

Attention

The purpose of persuasive writing is to capture attention. Without attention from your audience, the rest of your message may never be seen or heard (Sellers, 2022). It's essential to use bold statements or questions that immediately engage the reader to grab this initial attention. For instance, consider the headline "Are You Ready to Transform Your Life?" This question not only piques curiosity but also prompts an internal dialogue that makes the reader want to know more. Such phrasing hooks readers instantly by promising something valuable and out of the ordinary.

Interest

You can keep the audience engaged while presenting important information through compelling narratives. Stories have a unique power; they create emotional connections and make the content relatable. A marketer writing about a skincare product might share a story of someone who struggled with skin issues and found relief using the product. Thus, real-life scenarios resonate more than abstract claims, making the content memorable. Additionally, the information should be presented in a way that feels fresh and relevant, perhaps by highlighting trends or new research that supports the product's benefits.

Desire

Creating desire is where the magic of persuasion truly unfolds. This phase involves showcasing the benefits of your product or service and aligning these with the values and needs of your audience. It's not just about listing features; it's about painting a picture of a better future with your product at its center (Sellers, 2022). If you're advertising an eco-friendly car, emphasize the personal benefits, such as fuel efficiency and cost savings, alongside broader impacts like reducing carbon footprint. Connecting these benefits to what the audience values—cost-efficiency and environmental responsibility—will make the product much more desirable and appealing to your audience. Testimonials and social proof can further strengthen this phase by showing real-world examples of satisfied customers enjoying these benefits.

Action

Finally, encouraging action involves outlining clear next steps and offering incentives when appropriate. Once you've built up the reader's desire, it's paramount to make it easy for them to act on it (Sellers, 2022). Calls to action (CTAs) should be direct and unambiguous. Phrases like "Sign Up Now for a Free Trial" or "Buy Today to Get 20% Off" provide explicit instructions and incentives, nudging the audience toward conversion. These CTAs remove any barriers to action, such as uncertainty or reluctance, by providing value and clarity. It's beneficial to outline the steps, ensuring the audience knows exactly how to proceed and what they stand to gain by doing so.

Throughout the application of AIDA, maintaining a conversational tone helps make your message accessible and relatable. Imagine you're having a face-to-face discussion with your reader; this keeps the prose engaging and humanizes the brand behind it. Avoid complex jargon or overly technical descriptions to ensure your message doesn't alienate any potential customers. Simple, modern language allows your points to resonate more strongly with diverse audiences.

Use Secret Words That Convert

Persuasive writing involves powerful words. These are not ordinary words; they are carefully chosen terms that tap into deep-seated human desires and emotions. To truly leverage their potential, must recognize which words evoke emotional responses and how to weave them seamlessly into your narrative.

Power Words

Power words are like triggers in the mind; they create immediate emotional reactions. Words such as "exclusive" and "guaranteed" often evoke feelings of privilege and assurance (Haim, 2023). When a customer sees a product labeled as "exclusive," it suggests an offer that's not available to everyone, appealing to a desire for uniqueness or status. Similarly, the word "guaranteed" instills confidence, assuring the reader of a risk-free decision. These words are powerful because they align with common psychological desires and fears, offering solace or excitement where appropriate.

Effective Phrasing

While identifying power words is crucial, crafting effective phrases to spur action requires skillful phrasing and direct language use. The importance of keeping the language simple and precise cannot be overstated. Directness cuts through the clutter, making it easier for readers to understand and engage with your message. For instance, instead of saying, "Consider purchasing this product now," a phrase like "Buy now and save!" is more compelling. It uses clear, action-oriented language that leaves little room for hesitation. In crafting such phrases, brevity and clarity play pivotal roles, ensuring the reader knows exactly what is expected of them.

Contextual Usage

Understanding the context in which these words are used further enhances the impact of your message. Contextual usage means tailoring your words to suit the situation and audience, thus maximizing their effect. This involves knowing your audience well enough to predict what appeals to them. For example, using assertive language might work well in a high-energy sales pitch but could come across as aggressive in a more informative setting. Personalizing content ensures that your words resonate more deeply with the reader, making them feel understood and valued (Haim, 2023).

Contextualizing power words can be invaluable. To do so, start by identifying your audience's needs and preferences through market research or feedback. Once you have a clear picture, adapt your language to reflect this understanding. If your target audience values sustainability, incorporating words like "eco-friendly" or "sustainable choice" can make your copy more appealing. Always keep in mind the cultural and social nuances—what works for one group may not necessarily translate well for another.

Cultural Sensitivity

In today's global marketplace, adapting your language for cultural sensitivity is not just a nice-to-have; it's a necessity. Using culturally sensitive words ensures inclusivity and relevance, which, in turn, widens your appeal (Abdullah, 2024). Language that is considerate of cultural differences reflects an environment of respect and openness, which can lead to higher conversion rates. This means being aware of phrases or idioms that might not translate well across different cultures or might even offend certain demographics.

You can learn more about cultural sensitivity by conducting thorough research to understand the backgrounds, customs, and preferences of your target demographics. This effort will inform word choices that are both effective and considerate. For example, while humor can be a strong element in engaging writing, jokes or popular references in one culture might fall flat or be inappropriate in another. Tailoring your copy to acknowledge these nuances can significantly enhance its reception and effectiveness.

The journey to mastering persuasive copywriting is ongoing, marked by continuous learning and adaptation. The copy becomes more than just text—it transforms into a powerful tool for connection and conversion thanks to the use of power words, action phrases, contextual usage, and cultural sensitivity. Remember, persuasion isn't solely about using the right words; it's also about connecting with your audience's core beliefs and aspirations. Regardless of your motives to unleash the power of persuasive writing, the words you choose can be the difference between fleeting interest and meaningful engagement.

Understand Reciprocity Effects on Buying Behavior

The principle of reciprocity taps into an innate social tendency: When someone does something for us, we feel compelled to return the favor. Reciprocity is powerful because it influences decision-making and engenders a sense of trust between parties, making it an excellent tool for enhancing persuasive copywriting skills.

Reciprocity Principle

The reason behind this successful strategy lies in understanding how people feel obligated to repay favors (Adam, 2023). It's a deeply rooted psychological phenomenon observed across cultures and societies. Imagine being offered a gift or assistance—there's a natural inclination to reciprocate. This innate sense of duty creates a bond between the giver and receiver, reinforcing social cohesion.

In marketing, this behavior becomes particularly useful. You can establish a strong foundation of goodwill and trust that fosters future transactions by giving something of tangible value, such as free samples, informative resources, or personalized support at the outset. Interestingly, such acts of generosity induce a positive emotional response and a sense of indebtedness, prompting customers to engage further, ultimately leading to enhanced loyalty and increased sales. Imagine boosting your sales in exchange for giving away gifts to your customers. The good thing about this strategy is that it's also beneficial in the long run: People will always remember how you made them feel. Thus, leveraging the principle of reciprocity is not just a clever tactic but a strategic investment in building lasting relationships with consumers.

Creating Value

Offering free valuable content is a brilliant strategy to leverage this sentiment. I'm sure you're familiar with downloadable resources, free trials, or insightful articles. Consider doing the same with your audience. Value creation works because these offerings establish a positive initial impression. When individuals perceive genuine value without the immediate expectation of return, they are more likely to thank you through loyalty and purchases down the line (Adam, 2023). This approach opens up lines of communication and nurtures relationships that can be sustained over time.

A simple guideline in creating valuable content might include identifying your target audience's core needs or pain points. Focus on delivering solutions or insights that are directly beneficial, ensuring relevance.

Long-Term Effects

Building long-term brand loyalty revolves around sustained reciprocity efforts. It's essential to keep demonstrating value beyond initial interactions. Strive to be consistent in offering value to reinforce customer relationships and amplify a sense of loyalty. Brands that frequently provide useful information, exclusive offers, or personalized experiences are more likely to maintain their customers' interest. Over time, clients begin to see these brands as partners in their journey rather than just vendors. The magic of sustained reciprocity lies in its cumulative effect; each act of giving reinforces the customer's commitment to reciprocate through continued patronage (Krunal Vaghasiya, 2024).

Social Proof

The integration of social proof serves as a compelling enhancer of marketing credibility. The social proof relies on the idea that individuals look to others to guide their behaviors, especially in uncertain scenarios. If prospective customers witness testimonials from satisfied users or endorsements from influencers, they are more inclined to trust the product or service (Krunal Vaghasiya, 2024). This can be seen when existing customers share their positive experiences voluntarily and become brand advocates, enhancing your brand's image.

Showcasing expertise through free samples or consultations can be advantageous for attracting and retaining clients. For instance, a freelance writer might offer complimentary advice on crafting compelling narratives, thereby illustrating value upfront. Such gestures inspire potential clients to reciprocate by hiring services, appreciating that the initial engagement came without conditions attached.

Interestingly, the principle of reciprocity is not limited to large gestures; even small acts can engender significant influence. Simple thank-you notes or acknowledging a follower's thoughtful comment can prompt a reciprocal response, strengthening connection and engagement. The art of leveraging this principle involves sincerity and authenticity, steering clear of manipulation, which could otherwise backfire.

The principle of reciprocity works best when it feels natural and uncontrived. Audiences today are discerning and can easily detect disingenuous intentions. Authentic and consistent application of the reciprocity principle builds lasting relationships, while opportunistic attempts are likely to erode trust.

Balance Logical Appeal With Emotional Persuasion

Striking a balance between rational arguments and emotional appeals is the best way to reach a wider audience and obtain diverse perspectives. Each method has its strengths, but when effectively combined, they can significantly enhance the persuasive power of any message.

On the other hand, each method possesses its unique strengths, and when effectively combined, they create a harmonious interplay that significantly amplifies the persuasive power of any message. When you integrate logic with emotion, you can appeal to both the analytical thinkers who seek concrete evidence and the emotionally driven individuals who respond to storytelling and personal connections.

Logical Structure

Logical arguments in copywriting appeal to analytical customers who value evidence-based decision-making. Rational arguments provide the logical foundation that supports a message to inform and persuade audiences through intellectual understanding. Constructing these arguments involves using data, facts, and testimonials. For instance, if you're promoting a tech gadget, highlighting its specifications, efficiency, and user testimonials can help build a compelling case. Logical reasoning offers clarity and precision by presenting verifiable information that strengthens the argument's credibility. A graph or chart showing improvements over previous models or comparisons with competitors can also help visualize these logical points. This not only supports factual claims but also provides analytical minds with the tangible evidence they seek.

Emotional Resonance

Logic alone cannot persuade all customers. Emotions play a significant role in human decision-making, often influencing our choices more than we might realize. This is where storytelling becomes a powerful technique. Emotional appeals tap into the heart of human experience, evoking feelings of empathy, joy, fear, or passion that nurture a deeper connection with the audience. By weaving narratives that harness the power of feelings and emotions, you can connect with your audience on a profound level (Clickable, 2023). Imagine telling the story of a small business owner who overcame tough challenges due to a particular service; such narratives resonate emotionally, providing context and relatability that raw data cannot.

Creating Balance

A harmonious blend of logic and emotion ensures that your message appeals to both the mind and heart. For instance, consider an advertisement for a fitness program. While showcasing statistics about weight loss success rates (logic), you could also share personal stories of participants who regained confidence and improved their quality of life (emotion). This approach addresses different aspects of human behavior, making the copy more inclusive and impactful. This dual approach enriches the overall communication and ensures that the message appeals to a broader demographic. Using this balanced strategy results in gaining engagement, enhancing retention, and cultivating a sense of trust and connection, which are essential elements in persuading a diverse audience.

Audience Preferences

Different audiences have varied needs and respond differently to persuasive techniques. Tailoring your message to align with these preferences maximizes effectiveness. When you align your message with your target audience's unique characteristics and desires, you can enhance engagement and create a more compelling narrative. For example, if you're targeting a tech-savvy audience, focusing on technical specifications and innovative features may prove effective, as they are likely to prioritize functionality and cutting-edge advancements. Conversely, for an audience drawn to lifestyle benefits, emphasizing a product's experiential and transformative aspects might resonate more. This group may be more inclined to connect with stories that illustrate how the product can improve their everyday life or benefit personal growth.

Cultural Norms and Values

Tailoring emotional appeals requires sensitivity to cultural norms and values as well. Failing to account for these differences can result in messages that are not only ineffective but could also be perceived as insensitive or offensive. A multinational campaign, for instance, should consider local sentiments and cultural contexts to avoid messages that could be perceived as insensitive or ineffective. Just as humor or metaphors can work well in one culture, they may not translate effectively in another, potentially alienating rather than engaging the audience.

Moreover, cultural nuances extend beyond mere language; they encompass traditions, beliefs, and societal expectations that influence how individuals connect with messages on an emotional level. Acknowledging these complexities allows the design of emotionally charged campaigns that cultivate genuine engagement rather than alienation. Hence, it's important to carefully research and incorporate local culture into emotional appeals to demonstrate respect and appreciation for diverse audiences. This strategic approach improves your message and uplifts a deeper emotional bond with consumers, driving loyalty and encouraging positive perspectives across varied cultures.

Case Studies

To demonstrate this balance between rational arguments and emotional appeals, let's explore how various companies have achieved it. Apple, for instance, uses logical reasoning by detailing innovative features and offering customer testimonials about real-world experiences. They balance this with evocative visuals and stories that highlight creativity and personal empowerment, connecting deeply with their target market. Similarly, Tesla incorporates data-driven insights to demonstrate the superior performance of its vehicles, coupled with narratives about sustainable living, appealing to both logical consumers interested in technology and those motivated by environmental concerns.

To master this balance:

- Assess the primary appeal that resonates with your target audience—whether they respond more to data, stories, or a mix of both.

- Maintain clarity in presenting logical arguments; ensure that all facts are easily digestible and supported by credible sources.

- Craft emotional appeals with authenticity, avoiding manipulative or insincere tactics that might backfire.

- Regularly evaluate audience reactions to refine your approach and ensure your copy meets their evolving needs and preferences

Capitalize on Human Psychological Bias Toward Scarcity

Scarcity is a compelling principle in persuasive writing, mainly due to its profound psychological impact. At its core, scarcity is about human behavior and the intrinsic desire for things that seem limited or rare. This psychological trigger is often associated with the idea that perceived value increases when availability diminishes; when individuals believe something is scarce, they are more likely to see it as desirable and worthy of their attention.

The Scarcity Principle

This principle capitalizes on the idea that people are more motivated to act when they feel a resource is dwindling. It not only stirs an urgent response but also engages emotions, as people often associate rarity with quality and uniqueness. From concert tickets to exclusive memberships, making something appear scarce can significantly increase its perceived value and urgency.

Our brains are wired to respond quickly when we perceive a loss, a concept known as the loss aversion theory. Essentially, we feel the pain of losing something more acutely than the pleasure of gaining it. Thus, when an opportunity arises where scarcity is involved, such as a "limited edition" or "only a few left," our immediate reaction is often to seize the opportunity before it's too late. This urgency prompts quicker decision-making and boosts the likelihood of a purchase.

Ways to Implement the Scarcity Principle

To harness the power of these principles, create scenarios where consumers feel this urgency. One popular method is using countdown timers on promotions, which visually remind customers that time is running out (Agnew, 2024). This technique intensifies the impulse to buy and communicates a sense of finality. Similarly, restricted time frames, like flash sales that last just a day or a weekend, can drive immediate action from customers who might otherwise hesitate.

Another tactic is highlighting limited availability with phrases like "exclusive offers" or "members-only" access, tapping into consumers' fear of missing out (FOMO) and their desire to belong to an exclusive group. What's more, expressions like "limited edition" or "only a few left in stock" can immediately elevate interest and urgency, pushing potential customers to make quicker decisions out of concern for losing the opportunity altogether. For instance, brands like Supreme have mastered this approach by releasing products in limited quantities, creating hype and increasing demand with each new drop.

Sustaining Value

While scarcity can be a powerful motivator, ethical considerations cannot be overlooked. It's crucial to apply this principle responsibly. Artificially manipulating the availability of a product can backfire if customers realize the scarcity is manufactured. Transparency and honesty are key; ensuring that any claim of scarcity is genuine helps maintain consumer trust.

Moreover, from an ethical standpoint, it's important not to exploit vulnerable populations who may be more susceptible to pressure from scarcity tactics. You should aim to balance business interests with social responsibility, avoiding deceptive practices that mislead consumers. Ethical scarcity should guide potential customers to make informed decisions rather than pressuring them into actions they might later regret.

Long-Term Strategies

To build ongoing brand desirability, incorporating recurring scarcity offers can keep the excitement alive. This approach involves regularly introducing new, limited-time products or deals, maintaining a fresh appeal that continuously draws customers back.

Plus, long-term strategies using scarcity require maintaining a delicate balance between frequent offerings and retaining a sense of uniqueness (Agnew, 2024). While frequent scarcity offers can generate continued interest, overuse may dilute their effectiveness. A strategic approach could involve spacing out these offers and aligning them with key marketing events or seasons to maximize impact and anticipation.

Furthermore, cultivating a brand messaging that consistently emphasizes quality can complement scarcity tactics. When scarcity aligns with high-quality offerings, it solidifies the perception of premium value, as seen in luxury markets. Here, the allure isn't just in the rarity but in the association with excellence and prestige. Consumers often perceive scarce goods as superior, reinforcing brand loyalty and inviting repeat purchases.

To put these strategies into practice, here's what to keep in mind:

- Identify the aspects of your product or service that naturally lend themselves to scarcity–perhaps through limited production capacity or unique features.

- Communicate clearly why these items are rare, promoting appreciation for their exclusivity. Meanwhile, ensure transparency so consumers understand they're engaging with authentic scarcity.

- Use customer feedback to enhance future scarcity campaigns. Listening to how consumers respond to various offers can provide insights into what creates the most value, allowing adjustments to maintain attractiveness without compromising integrity.

Summary and Reflections

As we wrap up this chapter, we've explored how using well-established persuasion methods can significantly enhance your copywriting skills. With the AIDA formula, you've learned to grab attention, cultivate interest, build desire, and prompt action in a structured manner, ensuring that your messages are both engaging and effective. We also discovered the use of powerful words, which amplify your content by tapping into readers' emotions, creating an immediate connection. And don't forget the psychological principle of reciprocity, where offering value upfront makes customers more inclined to engage further. Together, these elements enrich your writing, allowing you to craft compelling narratives that resonate with various audiences, including marketers, business owners, and freelancers.

Besides, balancing logical appeal with emotional persuasion was highlighted as a critical skill. By marrying facts and figures with storytelling, you can reach different types of readers—those who seek evidence and those driven by emotion. This chapter also examined the importance of scarcity in copywriting, where showcasing limited availability can spur immediate action. However, remember to apply this principle honestly to maintain trust. Each technique discussed is a tool in your copywriting toolkit designed to help you communicate effectively and foster connections with your audience. As you continue developing these skills, let them guide you in crafting persuasive, authentic content that reflects your style and understanding of what truly captivates and converts.

Chapter 9:

Optimizing for SEO

Optimizing for SEO is a dynamic journey that blends art with science, where mastering the right techniques can significantly amplify your online presence. In an age dominated by digital interactions, having great content isn't enough if it remains hidden from your target audience. Understanding and implementing effective SEO strategies ensures your message doesn't just exist; it thrives in search engine results, reaching the people you most want to engage.

Throughout this chapter, we will explore the significance of keywords as a foundational element of SEO, revealing how they can be woven naturally into copy without compromising creativity or readability. You'll discover ways to position these keywords strategically within your content's structure, enhancing its appeal both to human eyes and search algorithms. We'll also examine the importance of content hierarchy—organizing information with clear headings and subheadings to maintain reader interest while boosting SEO efficiency. Furthermore, the chapter highlights innovative tactics like using long-tail keywords to capture niche audiences and balancing primary with secondary keywords for a coherent narrative. Finally, we'll cover practical aspects such as internal linking to improve site navigation and authority, ensuring your crafted messages attract attention and retain attention, and driving home their full persuasive potential.

Use Keywords Naturally in Copy

Incorporating keywords into writing is a fine art that balances the strength of SEO with the craft of engaging content. Mastering this method requires a deep understanding of relevant keywords and phrases that potential readers or customers are likely to search for and an appreciation for how to integrate them seamlessly into the narrative without ruining its natural flow.

Keyword Research Tools

The process begins with understanding how critical keyword research tools are in identifying appropriate keywords for your content. Tools like Google Keyword Planner, Ahrefs, and SEMrush are valuable here. These platforms help discern what potential audiences are searching for by offering data on search volume, competition levels, and keyword difficulty.

The use of such tools allows you to adjust content with search intent. For instance, if you're targeting small business owners looking to improve their digital marketing, you might discover through keyword research that phrases like "digital marketing tips for small businesses" have high search volume but moderate competition. This insight provides a great starting point for content creation, ensuring you use the right keywords that engage with your audience while also considering how difficult it will be to rank for those terms effectively.

Keyword Placement Strategies

Once you've chosen your keywords, the next step consists of positioning them naturally within your content. This starts with integrating them into key areas like titles, headers, and early paragraphs. Placing your primary keyword near the beginning of a title tag helps with SEO rankings (Hurley Hall, 2018) and makes the headline more enticing, drawing in clicks. For example, if your primary keyword is "organic skincare," an article titled "Organic Skincare: Essential Tips for Glowing Skin" positions your keyword prominently yet naturally.

What's more, placing your keywords on headers and sub-headings is also worthwhile. They act as signposts for readers and search engines, indicating the structure and topics covered in your content. Hence, using keywords in H1, H2, or H3 tags can significantly enhance SEO impact without hampering readability. Nevertheless, it's important to make sure these placements feel organic. Overstuffing headings with keywords can disrupt the flow and make content appear forced or awkward, which detracts from the user experience.

One effective strategy that often flies under the radar is leveraging long-tail keywords. These are longer, more descriptive phrases that reflect specific search queries frequently used by users closer to making a decision. Phrases like "best organic face creams for dry skin" cater to niche audiences seeking particular solutions, thus attracting a more qualified audience. Long-tail keywords generally enjoy lower competition and higher conversion rates, making them excellent for improving click-through rates and engagement metrics.

Content Relevance

Balancing primary and secondary keywords throughout the text is another layer of this nuanced approach. Primary keywords are those that most closely define your content's core topic, while secondary keywords offer supporting context. Strategically dispersing these throughout your writing ensures that the text remains coherent and natural. For instance, if your primary keyword is "digital marketing strategies," secondary keywords might include "online advertising" or "social media growth."

Achieving this balance prevents keyword stuffing—a practice frowned upon by both search engines and readers. Instead, it encourages a seamless integration where keywords enhance rather than hinder the narrative. This way, content remains focused on delivering value to the reader, upholding quality and engagement.

Moreover, consider moderation when integrating keywords into your content. Excessive use of keywords, known as keyword stuffing, detracts from readability and can even lead to penalization by search engines (Growth Machine, 2024). It's also important to remember that search engines prioritize content that provides genuine value over keyword-dense prose.

Structure Content for Readability and Ranking

Optimizing content for search engines isn't only a process; it's a strategy for increasing visibility and engagement. One crucial aspect of this is structuring content in a way that appeals to both users and search engine algorithms. This makes it easy to absorb information while also incorporating relevant keywords, headers, and metadata that search engines use to index and rank content.

Using Headings and Subheadings

At the heart of engaging content are headings and subheadings. These elements break text into manageable sections, providing a clear structure for readers to follow. For search engines, headings serve as key indicators of the content hierarchy and main topics discussed on a page. When incorporating relevant keywords into your headings, you enhance your page's SEO potential while making it easier for readers to navigate. Imagine browsing a lengthy article without any visual cues; it's easy to lose interest. However, with well-placed headings, readers can quickly identify sections of interest or importance. This keeps them engaged and can reduce bounce rates, a crucial metric for SEO.

Bullet Points and Lists

Beyond headings, bullet points and lists are helpful to simplify complex information. They allow you to present data succinctly and clearly, making it effortless for readers to grasp the main ideas without sifting through dense paragraphs. When deciding between a long paragraph and a list, consider how each would look from a reader's perspective. Lists are often more inviting and less intimidating to approach. Furthermore, search engines like Google sometimes use these lists directly in search results as snippets, offering another layer of visibility for your content.

Paragraph Length and Sentence Structure

Continuing with readability, the use of short paragraphs and sentences cannot be overstated. Long, winding sentences can deter readers, causing them to abandon a page prematurely. In contrast, concise sentences keep the reader's attention, enabling quick comprehension of the material. It's also beneficial to vary sentence length. A steady rhythm of similar-length sentences can become monotonous. Interspersing shorter and longer sentences adds dynamism, making the writing feel more natural and engaging. Remember, online readers often skim rather than read every word, so adapting your writing style to accommodate this behavior is crucial for maintaining their interest.

Internal Linking Practices

Internal linking is the practice of hyperlinking one page of a website to another page within the same website. By strategically placing links within your content, you guide readers to related topics, enhancing their understanding of the broader subject. For instance, if you have an article about digital marketing strategies, linking to another post about SEO tactics will provide readers with additional context and resources. Internally linked pages share 'link equity' among them, improving individual page authority and overall site strength (Ali, 2024). It's essential to ensure each link is accompanied by unique and descriptive anchor text to maintain clarity for users and search engines. Avoid using identical anchor texts leading to different pages, which could confuse users and negatively impact SEO.

Creating content hubs is a valuable internal linking strategy. Imagine a central hub page dedicated to a comprehensive topic, such as digital marketing, with numerous links to focus areas like SEO, content marketing, and social media. This setup directs users to relevant information and helps search engines comprehend the relationships between various content pieces, creating a robust architecture that supports SEO growth (Moz, n.d.).

Strategic Internal Links

Also, distributing your content's 'SEO value' through strategic internal links is valuable. High-authority pages on your site can lend credibility and visibility to lower-ranked pages, helping them rise in search engine rankings. Linking popular articles to newer or less visited pages contributes towards a cohesive site structure while encouraging exploration. This practice not only boosts the lesser-known pages' ranking potential but enriches user interaction by presenting diverse pathways through your site's content.

While building your internal linking strategy, be mindful of crawl depth. Ensure essential pages are easily accessible from the homepage within a few clicks. An intuitive, shallow clicking hierarchy simplifies navigation for visitors and search engines, facilitating better indexing and user satisfaction. The optimal website architecture resembles a pyramid, where information flows down from the homepage to category pages and subcategories, effectively organizing the site's content.

Navigational links found in menus or footers differ from contextual links embedded within content, yet both play significant roles. Navigational links offer straightforward paths to major site areas, whereas contextual links add depth, connecting relevant pages and enriching the user's learning journey.

Content Relevance to Keywords

Ensuring that your content matches chosen keywords is advantageous not only for visibility but also to truly resonate with your audience. When writing, strive to develop content that doesn't stop at addressing user queries superficially but dives into understanding and fulfilling the underlying search intent behind those queries. Search intent, or the 'why' behind a search, helps you create content that isn't merely informative but genuinely engaging.

Identifying The Needs of Your Audience

Think about the specific needs your audience might have when they search using particular keywords. Are users looking for detailed explanations, quick answers, or perhaps comparisons? Crafting your content to align with these motivations showcases your deep understanding of their needs, leading to higher satisfaction and increased dwell time on your site (Hardwick, 2019). For instance, if a keyword suggests the user is in an early research phase, offer comprehensive guides or how-to articles that can position you as a go-to resource.

Using Synonyms and Related Terms

Now, let's talk about expanding your content beyond those exact keywords. Utilization of synonyms and related terms can be advantageous. Here's why: This strategy not only enriches your content but also ensures your text remains captivating yet pertinent to a variety of potential searches. That way, using diverse vocabulary keeps your audience engaged and demonstrates a thorough grasp of the topic while enhancing your SEO quality.

Offering Value-Driven Content

High-quality copy is the backbone of effective content alignment. Focusing on crafting messages that offer clear value and relevance is significant. Whenever your audience feels they're genuinely learning or benefiting from your content, they're more likely to stay longer on your pages and return for more (Hardwick, 2019). In turn, this reduces bounce rates—a key indicator of a productive website. To achieve this, consider using structured storytelling. Narratives that weave solutions, case studies, or client testimonials within the copy naturally draw readers in, sparking curiosity and connection.

Engaging Narratives

Beyond conveying information, your content should promote interaction and satisfaction. Engaging narratives compel users to immerse, interact via comments or shares, and ultimately feel satisfied with their visit. Consider leveraging real-life examples or anecdotes that add personal touches to your writing. These elements help transform dry facts into lively discussions and relatable experiences. In doing so, you're more than just another source of information—you are offering a unique voice and perspective.

Thoughtfully crafted links connecting related content pieces across your site significantly enhance user navigation and boost engagement metrics. Internal linking acts like breadcrumbs, leading users through a well-curated journey of discovery, which can directly impact your site's authority and improve overall SEO outcomes.

Summary and Reflections

In this chapter, we've examined the essential strategies for enhancing your copy's visibility through effective SEO practices. Your writing can reach a broader audience thanks to the art of natural keyword integration and optimizing content structure. Using tools like Google Keyword Planner and SEMrush helps you identify key phrases that align with search intent, ensuring your material resonates with readers while also appealing to search engines. Remember, strategic keyword placement in titles, headers, and throughout the text should feel seamless, adding value to your narrative without sacrificing readability.

As you refine your content, consider how it meets the needs of your varied audiences. Also, emphasize balance by using long-tail keywords for specific queries and leveraging internal linking to enrich the reader's journey. Remember, the goal is visibility *and* engagement; building compelling stories and offering genuine insights will help keep your audience engaged.

Chapter 10:

Testing and Refining Your Copy

Testing and refining your copy is an ongoing journey in the realm of copywriting. At its essence, it's about understanding what resonates with audiences and transforming the way messages are delivered to enhance impact. Currently, crafting compelling content isn't enough; the true challenge lies in continuously testing and refining your work to ensure it captivates and converts.

Imagine a world where every word written has been meticulously evaluated through tried-and-tested methods to reach its utmost potential. This chapter invites you into that world, where rigorous testing methods and analytical insights come together to elevate copywriting from good to exceptional. We will explore a variety of testing techniques, such as A/B testing, which allows for informed decisions based on actual user interactions. Furthermore, the chapter covers how leveraging analytics tools provides critical insights into audience behavior, helping adapt strategies to remain relevant in changing environments. You'll learn to measure effectiveness by tracking key performance indicators (KPIs) and establishing benchmarks that align with marketing goals. Most importantly, embracing a mindset that welcomes iteration is the secret to viewing feedback as a stepping stone toward perfection.

From analyzing statistical significance to adapting strategies based on metrics, the insights provided aim to create a high-impact copy. This exploration promises not only to sharpen your skills but also to inspire a new appreciation for the power of refined copy that speaks directly to your intended audience.

Conduct A/B Testing to Compare Versions

Understanding what your audience truly responds to is the secret to successful copy. A/B testing is one of the most effective methods for determining which copy resonates best with your audience. Let's take a more in-depth look at this subject, recognizing A/B testing as a tool and a key strategy for identifying optimal content solutions.

Understanding A/B Testing

At its core, A/B testing—or split testing—entails comparing two versions of a piece of content to see which performs better (Kolowich, 2018). For example, you might have two different headlines for an email; Version A might use one phrasing while Version B uses another. Presenting each version to a similar audience segment lets you gather insights into which headline engages more effectively. The results gained from such tests are invaluable in refining the effectiveness of marketing materials, making A/B testing indispensable in the marketer's toolkit.

The primary advantage of A/B testing is that it provides data-backed insights rather than relying on assumptions about what audiences might prefer. While intuition and creative instincts play significant roles in copywriting, they are susceptible to personal biases and misconceptions. In contrast, A/B testing offers concrete evidence showing how real users interact with different versions of a message (Maku Seun, 2023). This evidence-based approach allows them to move beyond guesswork and make informed decisions that enhance the quality and impact of their content.

One of the significant findings from A/B testing is that even small changes can lead to substantial differences in performance. Consider a scenario where simply altering the color or text of a call-to-action button results in increased click-through rates. Such minor adjustments might seem insignificant during the planning phase but can hugely impact user engagement and conversion metrics.

Choosing Variables To Test

An essential aspect of successful A/B testing is deciding which elements of the copy to test. It's important to focus on areas with the potential to influence user behavior significantly (Kolowich, 2018). You might choose to test specific features like tone, wording, layout, or imagery. Testing different tones can reveal whether a formal or casual voice aligns better with the target demographic. Alternatively, experimenting with word choice can determine whether certain phrases generate higher engagement levels.

To illustrate how these concepts manifest in practice, consider a business that wants to improve its landing page performance. The team decided to conduct an A/B test focusing on the primary message displayed. Version A maintains the current, concise, straightforward statement, whereas Version B attempts a longer, more detailed explanation. Upon completion, the results indicate that visitors engage more with the concise message, possibly due to clarity and directness. Consequently, the business adapts this approach across other campaigns, witnessing improved engagement consistently.

When implementing A/B tests, you must run each test simultaneously among random audience groups to minimize external factors affecting outcomes. Running the experiments concurrently ensures that variations in timing or audience characteristics don't skew the data. Additionally, determining an adequate sample size is critical for acquiring reliable results.

A necessary consideration when analyzing A/B test results is to confirm the statistical significance of the data, which should guide strategic decisions. Once valid conclusions are drawn, winning elements from successful tests should be implemented across broader campaigns.

Utilize Analytics Tools for Insights

Understanding how well your copy performs entails leveraging analytical tools that help uncover that information. Let's examine the benefits and methodologies for utilizing these tools to gather insights so you can enhance your content strategy:

Overview of Analytics Tools

Initially, it's crucial to familiarize yourself with a variety of analytics tools available at your disposal. These tools collect key metrics necessary for measuring how your copy resonates with your audience. Engagement rates and conversions are two primary metrics. Engagement rates indicate how well your audience connects with your content—whether they find it compelling enough to engage further or share it (Chakraborty, 2023). Conversions go a step deeper, revealing whether your copy successfully persuades the audience to take a desired action, such as signing up for a newsletter or making a purchase.

Data Interpretation

Interpreting this data is another critical component of leveraging analytics. By understanding how to read these metrics, you can discern not only the level of engagement your copy achieves but also the nuances of writing success. For instance, a high engagement rate coupled with a low conversion rate might suggest that while your copy catches attention, it may not be persuasive enough to drive actions. Conversely, a high conversion rate could indicate impactful messaging, but if engagement is low, there might be barriers preventing broader audience interaction (Fiveable, 2024).

Analyzing these patterns allows you to spot trends over time, which can be instrumental in informing future copy strategies. Consider a scenario where you notice a consistent drop in engagement every time specific topics are covered. This trend suggests those subjects may not resonate well with your target audience, prompting a revision of your content focus. Similarly, identifying what works can guide you in amplifying successful themes, tones, or calls to action.

Setting Measurable Goals

Furthermore, setting and adjusting goals based on these insights can profoundly refine your copywriting approach. With data-driven insights, it's possible to set realistic and strategic objectives that align closely with actual audience behavior and preferences. For example, if past data reveals a peak in engagement during certain campaigns, replicating elements from these successful endeavors in new contexts could boost performance. Continuously adjusting your goals according to the latest analytics ensures your strategies remain relevant and effective.

Let's consider an example to illustrate these points. Suppose an online retailer analyzes their email marketing campaign performance using a tool like Google Analytics. They observe through engagement metrics that emails sent on Thursdays have higher open rates, suggesting their customers are more engaged towards the weekend. They also note a spike in conversions when promotional discount codes are included within the first three lines of the email content. Armed with this data, they can strategize future campaigns to optimize open rates by timing them closer to weekends and ensuring call-to-action prompts appear early in the communication.

Adapting Strategy Based on Analytics

Analytical insights are the starting point for continuously refining copy strategies. You can maintain alignment with shifting market dynamics and evolving consumer expectations through ongoing evaluation and adjustment. These practices bolster a responsive and agile marketing strategy that consistently meets audience needs and maximizes communication impact (Fiveable, 2024).

There are widely used analytical software options that support this process. Platforms like HubSpot Marketing Analytics and Google Analytics offer comprehensive dashboards and reports tailored to track and measure various marketing efforts. These tools extend capabilities beyond basic metric tracking, enabling event tracking, revenue attribution, and more—all designed to paint a holistic picture of marketing performance.

Ultimately, leveraging analytics is about creating a feedback loop. Metrics guide the refinement of strategies, which, in turn, are tested against real-world outcomes, enabling continuous improvement. As you engage with these practices, remember it's not just about collecting data; it's about understanding what that data tells you about your audience and how to use it to craft messages that captivate and compel. Analytics turns raw numbers into actionable insights, bridging the gap between potential and performance.

Track and Measure Key Performance Indicators

Monitoring key performance indicators (KPIs) is fundamental in evaluating and enhancing the effectiveness of copywriting efforts. KPIs provide a clear picture of how well the writing aligns with business objectives. They serve as measurable values that help determine whether marketing strategies are driving desired outcomes, such as increased sales, enhanced customer engagement, or improved brand awareness.

Identifying Relevant KPIs

To begin with, it's essential to introduce relevant KPIs that assess the impact of copywriting on business goals. For instance, in digital marketing campaigns, click-through rates (CTR), conversion rates, and return on ad spend (ROAS) are key indicators of success. These metrics measure the ability of copy to attract clicks, convert visitors into customers, and generate revenue surpassing advertising costs. Similarly, in email marketing, open rates signify the effectiveness of subject lines, while click-through rates indicate the compelling nature of the call-to-action within emails.

Setting Benchmarks for KPIs

Establishing benchmarks and realistic expectations for KPI measurement involves analyzing past performance data and aligning future targets with overarching business goals (Hall, 2024). Recognizing industry standards and past achievements helps create achievable goals that propel your copy forward. For example, setting a CTR target based on previous high-performing campaigns provides a realistic aim that motivates continual improvement. Adopting SMART goals—specific, measurable, achievable, relevant, and time-bound—ensures that KPI objectives are clearly defined and strategically aligned.

Analyzing KPI Trends

Once KPIs are established, interpreting trends over time can refine strategic improvements in copywriting. Consistent monitoring of KPI data reveals insights into long-term trends, such as seasonal shifts in consumer behavior or the sustained effectiveness of certain copy elements. For instance, noticing a decline in email open rates could prompt testing of new subject line styles or optimization of sending times. Conversely, a steady increase in social media engagement rates might suggest successful audience resonance, encouraging the reinforcement of similar content strategies. Understanding these trends allows us to proactively adjust strategies and capitalize on positive or correct negative patterns.

Reporting on KPI Performance

Effective reporting methods play a vital role in communicating KPI findings to your team. Visual representation of data, such as graphs and charts, helps convey complex information simply and effectively. Dashboards and concise reports summarize vital insights and highlight areas requiring attention or celebrating successes.

Examining the sentiment and themes within customer feedback, comments, or reviews helps contextualize numerical KPI results. This holistic view offers a deeper comprehension of how targeted audiences perceive and engage with the copy, providing invaluable insights for ongoing refinement.

Ultimately, tracking KPIs empowers data-driven decision-making, leading marketing strategies toward greater success. By identifying which elements of copy are performing well and which require improvement, resources and budgets can be optimally allocated to high-performing tactics.

Iterate Based on Testing Results

The iterative nature of refining copy is akin to the endless pursuit of perfection, where the journey itself brings growth and adaptation. At its core, continuous testing isn't a destination but an ongoing process that evolves alongside audience expectations and preferences (Fiveable, 2024b). Testing should be viewed as a vital component of success rather than a singular event; it's about creating a culture where learning and improvement are integral to everyday operations.

A Mindset of Growth

In embracing a growth mindset, we must recognize that feedback is not criticism but a pathway to betterment. Adopting a growth mindset requires letting go of the fear of failure and viewing each feedback piece as an opportunity for refinement. It involves actively seeking input from diverse sources, whether it comes from performance data or direct customer interactions.

Iterative Testing

Iterative testing serves as a bridge between today's results and tomorrow's innovation. As audience behaviors shift with societal trends, technological advancements, and platform changes, so must the messaging that captures their attention. Consider how seasonal fluctuations, current events, or emerging technologies might influence your audience's priorities. What resonated last year may become obsolete today, and staying attuned to these changes through iterative testing allows for content creation that feels fresh and engaging.

One of the greatest strengths of continuous iteration is its ability to adapt and thrive in ever-changing environments. This adaptability extends beyond merely tracking trends—it involves understanding why certain messages succeed. Iterative testing helps identify the nuances of what works, providing deeper insights into audience motivations and desires (Fiveable, 2024b). With this knowledge, you can tailor strategies to meet specific needs, ensuring their copy remains compelling and aligned with audience interests.

Past successes and failures should serve as guideposts for future endeavors. Each test result provides valuable lessons, illuminating paths taken and those left unexplored. Campaigns that have fallen short reveal areas for improvement, while successful initiatives offer blueprints for replicating triumphs.

This iterative approach encourages a proactive stance toward marketing, encouraging anticipation rather than reaction. Instead of waiting for issues to arise, you can preemptively address potential challenges by analyzing historical data and current trends. This forward-thinking strategy positions businesses to navigate industry shifts with agility and confidence.

A/B testing is one strategic method used in iterative processes, allowing multiple versions of copy to compete against each other to determine which performs best. Copywriters can refine messaging incrementally by carefully analyzing metrics such as click-through rates (CTR) or conversion rates. Testing minor variations, like headline phrasing or call-to-action wording, can yield significant improvements, often referred to as "marginal gains." Even subtle tweaks can have profound effects on engagement, illustrating the power of data-driven decision-making.

Understanding the iterative nature of refining copy involves recognizing that experimentation never truly ends. Just as technology and audience inclinations evolve, so must our approaches to crafting persuasive messages. The iterative cycle—test, learn, refine—becomes a rhythm that drives continual growth and advancement.

Summary and Reflections

As we've explored in this chapter, the key to creating compelling copy lies in a continuous process of testing and analyzing. Incorporating A/B testing into your strategy provides valuable insights into how small changes can significantly impact user engagement and conversion rates. This process moves beyond guesswork, providing concrete data that helps refine every aspect of your messaging, from headlines to call-to-action buttons. The attention to detail in these tests allows marketers, business owners, content creators, and freelancers alike to enhance the quality of their content and tailor it more precisely to meet audience expectations.

In conjunction with A/B testing, leveraging analytics tools offers an in-depth understanding of copy performance. These tools enable you to track various metrics like engagement and conversion rates, providing a clearer picture of what resonates with your audience. Being able to interpret this data helps identify trends and guide adjustments that ensure your content remains relevant and impactful. Together, testing and analytics create a dynamic framework for continuously iterating and improving your copywriting techniques.

Chapter 11:

Building Resilience

and Adaptability

Building resilience and adaptability in copywriting demands persistence and flexibility. In today's fast-paced market, it's crucial to be able to adjust strategies and approaches.

This chapter teaches you how to constructively incorporate feedback to fuel progress. Discover the art of learning from even the most challenging critiques, turning potential setbacks into stepping stones for growth. You'll also examine the necessity of embracing multiple revisions as a pathway to refining your craft. Next, we'll delve into the significance of establishing a sustainable feedback loop, highlighting how this practice ensures your writing evolves continually without stagnation. Finally, let's uncover the value of maintaining lifelong learning as an adaptable skill set in the ever-changing landscape of copywriting.

Incorporating Feedback Constructively

Feedback serves not only as a means to enhance one's skills but also as a mirror reflecting areas that might be overlooked. Often, when engrossed in writing, it's easy to get lost in one's narrative and style. Constructive feedback from peers, clients, or readers can unveil aspects of the work that could be strengthened or refined, providing a clearer path to improvement (Botta, 2024).

Understanding the Value of Constructive Criticism

Successful copywriters understand the value of feedback and actively seek it out to continuously refine their strategies. They recognize that remaining static in their approach can lead to stagnation. By engaging with feedback, they open themselves to evolving market conditions and client expectations.

Embracing constructive criticism promotes a growth mindset and encourages a culture of adaptability that is essential in today's fast-paced environment. Furthermore, embracing feedback can lead to the development of more innovative and compelling copy, as it encourages writers to experiment with new ideas, tones, and formats. This active pursuit of constructive criticism can lead to more innovative copy and strategic writing (Botta, 2024).

Implementing Feedback in Practical Ways

Once feedback is received, the next step is to conduct a systematic review and prioritization of actionable suggestions. Not all feedback is created equal; some may be highly relevant, while others might be less applicable. It's essential to distill the input into a list of actionable changes that can genuinely enhance writing quality. Therefore, it's imperative to approach the feedback with a discerning eye, evaluating the context and intent behind each suggestion. By categorizing feedback according to its relevance and potential impact, you can effectively distill the input into a concise list of actionable changes that can genuinely enhance the quality of your writing. This prioritization process not only streamlines the incorporation of feedback but also allows you to focus your efforts on the most critical areas for improvement. Additionally, strive to keep an open and flexible mindset to explore innovative ideas that might arise while considering suggested changes.

Establishing a Feedback Loop

Building a feedback loop is a fundamental strategy for cultivating consistent development and innovation. A feedback loop involves regularly seeking opinions, making adjustments, and revisiting the revised material for further evaluation. This iterative cycle of receiving, implementing, and assessing feedback cultivates a discipline that keeps copywriters aligned with industry standards and audience preferences.

Incorporating feedback loops into your writing routine promotes resilience. You learn to detach personal feelings from professional critiques, viewing each comment as an opportunity rather than a setback. When handled constructively, even seemingly harsh criticism can become a powerful tool for professional growth. With every iteration of the feedback loop, you are not just improving a single document but refining your entire skill set (Saad, 2024).

Consider the example of renowned authors and copywriters who reached the pinnacle of their careers through relentless perseverance and openness to critique. These individuals did not achieve success in isolation; instead, they thrived on the insights shared by editors, mentors, and peers. For instance, Stephen King famously revised his manuscripts multiple times, valuing the feedback from trusted advisers, which contributed significantly to the polished narratives you see today.

Building a Culture of Feedback

Furthermore, creating a culture of feedback within your team or organization can amplify the benefits of this approach. Encouraging an environment where feedback is readily given and received helps build a collaborative and supportive atmosphere. In such settings, your creativity flourishes, and innovative ideas are exchanged freely. You feel empowered to share your thoughts without fear of judgment, knowing that your input is valued and respected. This, in turn, leads to more dynamic and cohesive project outcomes.

However, embracing feedback requires a certain level of humility and vulnerability. It demands the acknowledgment that there is always room for improvement, regardless of your experience level. Hence, maintaining an open mind and a willingness to learn contributes to developing a robust skill set that adapts seamlessly to any changes.

Learning From Negative Feedback

The journey to mastering resilience begins with embracing feedback, no matter how negative it may seem at first. Critiques, especially the harsher ones, provide valuable learning opportunities that can significantly enhance your abilities over time.

Identifying Constructive Elements from Negative Feedback

The first step in this learning process involves identifying and extracting constructive elements from negative feedback. Instead of dismissing harsh reviews as mere criticism, view them as a chance to identify areas that require improvement (Saad, 2024). For example, if feedback highlights that your write-ups lack emotional appeal, take it as an opportunity to explore emotional triggers and integrate them into your work. Over time, this approach transforms perceived failures into catalysts for growth, gradually honing your skills and making you more adept at your craft.

Subjective Opinions vs. Constructive Suggestions

A key element in this transformative process is differentiating between subjective opinions and constructive suggestions. Negative commentary is often laced with personal biases or preferences that don't necessarily equate to facts. It's helpful to discern when feedback is merely someone's taste and when it provides actionable insights. Constructive suggestions typically come with examples or explanations that guide improvement. Focusing on these, rather than subjective criticism, can help to find direction in your learning journey and avoid confusion stemming from conflicting opinions.

Cultivating Persistence

Persistence in adapting through adversity is another fundamental aspect of building resilience in copywriting. Adversity is inevitable in any creative field, and the ability to persist despite challenges sets successful writers apart. This involves continually refining your work and adjusting strategies based on feedback. Persistence doesn't mean stubbornly adhering to one's ways but being open to evolution based on external inputs (Saad, 2024). Each adaptation enhances your current project and prepares you for future challenges, gradually building a robust foundation for resilient copywriting.

Normalizing Feedback

Feedback should not be seen as an attack on your capabilities but as part of a continuous learning cycle. Developing a habit of seeking regular feedback—be it from peers, clients, or mentors—and viewing it as a routine rather than an occasional event helps detach emotions from critiques (Bhavya Sri Khandrika, 2024). As feedback becomes a normalized practice, it shifts the focus from personal defensiveness to professional enhancement, paving the way for a positive learning experience.

Reflective Practices

Reflective practices give room to internalize lessons learned and strategize on implementing changes. Moreover, maintaining a journal of received feedback and subsequent actions taken can track progress over time, highlighting growth areas and persistent challenges (Saad, 2024). This reflective practice reinforces learned concepts and ensures they translate into enhanced writing quality.

In addition to individual efforts, seeking community support is vital in developing resilience against harsh critiques. Sharing experiences and receiving input from fellow copywriters or mentors provides new perspectives, advice, and encouragement. Engaging with a supportive network can make the feedback process less isolating and more interactive, offering emotional reassurance and practical guidance. Surround yourself with a community that understands the nuances of copywriting, and you'll be better equipped to face critiques with confidence and composure.

Lastly, it's important to remember that the path to adeptness in copywriting is a marathon, not a sprint. Growth derived from criticism is incremental and requires patience. Remain committed to adapting and learning from each piece of feedback, even the most critical, so you can cultivate a deep-rooted resilience that improves your writing and strengthens your capacity to handle any market changes. This resilience is invaluable in the ever-evolving world of copywriting.

Remaining Persistent through Multiple Revisions

In the dynamic world of copywriting, the art of crafting compelling messages is not born in a single draft but rather through the process of iterative refinement. High-quality copy often emerges from multiple drafts, each iteration refined and polished through valuable feedback and meticulous revision. This iterative process allows you to hone your ideas, clarify your messages, and ultimately produce content that resonates deeply with audiences.

The Importance of Revision in Writing

One of the cornerstones of successful iterative refinement in copywriting is understanding the significance of producing several drafts before arriving at a final version. By taking the time to revisit and revise your initial concepts, you can identify areas for improvement and explore alternative angles that might elevate your work. The feedback process provides fresh perspectives that challenge your assumptions and highlight overlooked opportunities. Feedback serves as a mirror, showcasing your draft's strengths and weaknesses and guiding you toward more effective communication strategies.

Strategies to Overcome the Frustration of Revision

As beneficial as revisions can be, they can also become a source of frustration for many writers. To manage this, make it a habit to set clear goals for each drafting stage. To do so, establish specific objectives—whether refining tone, enhancing clarity, or focusing on audience engagement—to maintain direction and momentum throughout the revision process (Fiveable, 2024b). These goals act as guideposts, providing a framework within which your creativity can flourish without becoming overwhelming. Structured goals serve as a compass amidst the uncertainty of your creative endeavors and keep your project aligned with its intended purpose.

Embracing Iterative Creativity

Iterative creativity is another powerful tool in your arsenal, enabling you to discover unique ideas and narrative angles even amidst challenges. Often, your first draft is merely an exploration of potential themes and messages; it is the subsequent iterations that reveal hidden gems. Learn to approach each draft as an opportunity for refinement and innovation, and encourage yourself to think outside the box and push beyond conventional boundaries (Fiveable, 2024b). This mindset transforms perceived setbacks into opportunities for advancement, building resilience and adaptability in the face of evolving market demands.

Building a Personal Revision Strategy

Personalizing a structured revision approach further enhances your innovation and persistence in copywriting. You have a unique style and workflow, meaning that a one-size-fits-all plan is unlikely to yield optimal results. Instead, tailoring the revision process to your individual preferences and strengths enables you to engage more deeply with your work. You might find value in collaborating with others and drawing inspiration from different viewpoints to refine your messaging. Alternatively, you might prefer solitude, allowing introspection to guide your revisions. Embracing a personalized approach will create an environment where your creativity can thrive and new ideas can take root.

Incorporating structured practices does not stifle your creativity; instead, it provides a stable foundation upon which your creativity can build (Fiveable, 2024b). For instance, incorporating brainstorming sessions into your drafting routine can spark innovative concepts that might otherwise remain undiscovered.

Iterative Refinement

Iterative refinement invites you to embrace failure as a stepping stone to success. Not every draft will hit the mark, but each attempt offers valuable lessons that contribute to your future improvements. This continuous learning cycle promotes a patient and open-minded perspective, empowering you to adapt your techniques in response to shifting consumer preferences and industry trends. Your willingness to iterate and refine separates you from the rest, as it demonstrates your commitment to delivering relevant and impactful content.

Ultimately, iterative refinement in copywriting is about crafting an authentic, persuasive, and emotionally resonant message (Fiveable, 2024b). By developing multiple drafts, welcoming constructive feedback, and employing goal-oriented strategies, you transform raw ideas into polished pieces that captivate and convert audiences.

Refinement is not solely a task for the solitary writer but a collaborative effort that benefits from diverse perspectives. Engaging with peers, mentors, or industry experts fosters a sense of community, where collective knowledge enriches your creativity. Such interactions help you challenge existing paradigms, explore uncharted territories, and stretch the limits of your imagination.

Staying Ahead With Lifelong Learning

In today's rapidly evolving market, being a successful copywriter demands a commitment to continuous learning. Engaging with industry trends, participating in workshops and webinars, dedicating time to reading, and leveraging the power of mentorship or peer groups all contribute to building your skillsets and keeping your content fresh and impactful.

Engaging With Industry Trends

The market landscape is dynamic, with consumer preferences and technological advancements constantly reshaping the playing field. Thus, tuning into these changes ensures your content remains relevant and engaging over time (Dennison, 2023). For example, understanding shifts in social media algorithms or emerging platforms can help content creators and marketers tailor their strategies to reach wider audiences effectively. Similarly, recognizing changes in consumer behavior can help adjust your messaging to better meet customer needs, thereby driving sales and fostering loyalty.

Participating in Workshops and Webinars

Workshops and webinars are valuable tools for your skill enhancement through continuous training and exposure. They provide opportunities for you to learn from industry experts and peers, offering new perspectives and techniques to apply to your work. For example, attending a webinar on persuasive writing techniques could help you refine your proposals or craft more compelling pitches as a freelancer or sales professional. Furthermore, because many workshops and webinars are now available online, they are accessible to a global audience, enabling you to gain insights from diverse cultures and markets without leaving your desk.

Reading and Researching Regularly

Regular reading enriches your knowledge and sparks fresh creative strategies, empowering you to innovate and adapt. You can delve into books, articles, and industry reports and uncover new ideas and approaches to incorporate into your work. Reading widely also broadens your understanding of various subjects, allowing you to write with authority and confidence across a range of topics.

Finding a Mentor or Peer Group

Engaging with others in your field offers a platform for exchanging feedback, discussing challenges, and celebrating successes. A mentor can provide guidance based on their experiences, helping you navigate complex situations and avoid potential pitfalls. On the other hand, peer groups offer opportunities for exchanges and mutual support, promoting a sense of belonging and motivation. For example, you might receive constructive criticism on your writing style from a peer group, leading to improvements and greater reader engagement. Similarly, collaborating with mentors might help you discover new avenues for client acquisition and project management.

The necessity of ongoing education cannot be overstated, particularly in a world where change is the only constant. Investing in your professional development not only sharpens your existing skills but also opens doors to new opportunities and career advancement.

Moreover, adaptability is a highly valued trait in today's unpredictable economy (Dennison, 2023). Employers increasingly seek candidates committed to professional development and upskilling. By embracing a growth mindset and actively pursuing educational opportunities, you position yourself as a valuable asset, capable of thriving amidst uncertainty and contributing meaningfully to organizational goals.

Summary and Reflections

In this chapter, we've explored how persistence and flexibility are vital skills in the ever-evolving world of copywriting for you. By embracing feedback as an opportunity for growth, you can adapt your craft to meet changing market demands and client expectations. Also, the process of constructive criticism helps illuminate areas for improvement, offering valuable insights that might go unnoticed otherwise. In addition, establishing a feedback loop ensures that iterative refinement becomes part of your writing routine, allowing you to continuously polish your work through regular reviews and input from peers or mentors. This not only enhances the quality of your pieces but also fosters your long-term professional development.

We've also highlighted the importance of lifelong learning and community support in mastering the art of persuasive writing for you. Staying informed about industry trends and engaging in ongoing education like workshops or reading opens the doors to opportunities. The collaborative aspect of feedback within a supportive network amplifies your creativity and innovation, encouraging you to explore fresh approaches and perspectives. Embracing this mindset of continuous improvement empowers you to thrive in ever-changing marketplaces.

Chapter 12:

Copywriting and Technology

Advancements

Copywriting's relationship with technology has continually evolved, but the advent of artificial intelligence (AI) marks a particularly transformative chapter in its development. AI is increasingly finding its way into the creative process, changing how copy is created and refined. The allure of this technological advancement is hard to ignore—machines that can decode human language, craft compelling messages, and even offer stylistic suggestions promise to make writing tasks quicker and potentially more precise.

As AI tools become more prevalent in copywriting, this chapter will explore the excitement and the complexity they bring. We will discover how AI balances efficiency with the need for personal touch—highlighting the ways it assists writers in overcoming creative blocks and freeing them from mundane tasks. Yet, there's an ethical side to consider since AI-driven content creation walks a fine line between innovation and artistic integrity. This chapter aims to illuminate the path forward for marketers, business owners, and creatives as they navigate the intersection of technology and persuasive communication, offering insights into leveraging AI without losing the human touch at the heart of effective storytelling.

Introduction to AI in Copywriting

Integrating AI in copywriting marks a significant evolution in how content is conceived and executed. At the forefront of this transformation are various AI technologies that have begun to redefine what is possible within the industry. This capability forms the backbone of modern AI applications in copywriting, where tasks previously requiring detailed human intervention can now be managed by sophisticated software.

AI-Powered Content Creation Tools

Tools like OpenAI's GPT-3 have revolutionized the writing process, enabling marketers and writers to generate high-quality drafts rapidly. These tools can sift through enormous datasets to produce text that closely mimics human writing styles, providing inspiration and laying substantial groundwork for content creators. With features that suggest improvements in tone, style, and structure, AI content creation tools not only expedite the initial drafting phase but also assist in enhancing creativity by freeing writers from routine tasks, allowing them to focus on crafting unique and compelling narratives. The ability of these tools to assist in generating ideas or combating writer's block exemplifies AI's role as both an enhancer of efficiency and a liberator of creativity.

AI-Driven SEO Solutions

SEO, a critical component of digital marketing strategies, also benefits significantly from AI integration. AI-driven SEO solutions offer capabilities far beyond traditional methods. For instance, they can analyze search engine algorithms and user behavior and help optimize content for better visibility and higher rankings. They also provide insights into trending keywords, suggest content adjustments, and even predict future search trends based on historical data analysis, thus ensuring the content remains relevant and competitive.

A New Hybrid Approach to AI

Traditionalists who have long relied on instinct and experience may initially view AI with skepticism. However, embracing AI does not mean abandoning established methods; instead, it allows for an augmentation of the creative process. AI tools can handle time-consuming tasks such as research and fact-checking, leaving more room for human writers to apply their expertise where it truly counts: in crafting messages that resonate emotionally and intuitively with audiences. This synergy between AI and human input illustrates a productive coexistence where each complements the other's strengths.

Balancing AI and Human Oversight

As this integration continues, it's vital to recognize that AI doesn't replace the need for human oversight. Instead, it reshapes roles within the content creation process. While AI can drive impressive efficiencies and uncover data-driven insights, it cannot replicate the nuanced understanding of cultural context and emotional depth that human writers bring. Thus, the successful deployment of AI in copywriting involves a balanced partnership—one where AI handles scalable functions and humans focus on strategic, heartfelt communication.

AI technologies are not static; they continuously evolve, becoming more intuitive and capable over time. Staying informed of these changes ensures you remain at the cutting edge, ready to leverage AI's full potential while maintaining the artfulness of your craft. This balance is essential for those seeking to excel in modern copywriting, where efficiency and creativity must coexist harmoniously.

Maximizing Efficiency through AI

Automation methods have begun to seamlessly integrate into your copywriting process, significantly reducing repetitive tasks and supporting you in focusing on more creative aspects of your work. Tools driven by AI can effortlessly handle routine operations such as proofreading, grammar checks, and even basic styling adjustments, saving significant amounts of time for you as a copywriter who these repetitive tasks would otherwise burden.

Automated Content Generation Systems

An exemplary implementation is automated content generation systems. These systems can create foundational drafts with minimal human intervention, setting a base for your further refinement and creativity. For instance, AI can quickly produce generic product descriptions or social media updates, which you can later customize to better align with brand-specific messaging. This initial groundwork reduces the heavy lifting for you and allows you to concentrate on fine-tuning and elevating the content quality.

AI's Editing and Reviewing Processes

Advanced AI algorithms, like those employed in spell-checkers and grammar tools, offer sophisticated analysis capabilities that extend beyond basic typographic errors. These tools assess syntax, tone, and even structure to ensure the message you deliver is coherent and precisely aligned with your intended communication goals. The quick feedback loop provided by AI accelerates your revision process and ensures high-quality output, reducing the need for multiple rounds of manual editing.

Data-Driven Insights

Furthermore, AI improves your decision-making through data-driven insights by harnessing vast datasets to analyze consumer behavior patterns. Algorithms can sift through massive amounts of data much faster than you can, identifying trends and preferences that might not be immediately obvious. Understanding these patterns is important to make informed decisions regarding content strategy and tailoring your copy to better match consumer expectations. Such data analytics can reveal what type of content resonates most with audiences, allowing you to craft messages that are both timely and relevant, ultimately improving engagement and conversion rates (Tumas, 2024).

For example, an AI-driven tool may detect increased interest in environmentally sustainable products among your target demographic.

Using this insight, you can focus your efforts on highlighting eco-friendly features in your marketing copy, appealing directly to consumer values and increasing the likelihood of positive responses. This insight-driven approach enhances the effectiveness of your marketing campaigns and refines the overall strategic direction of your content creation.

Integrating AI Into Your Workflow

A clear benefit of automation is its ability to streamline the management of project timelines and deadlines. By automating assignment reminders, progress tracking, and collaboration tools, AI allows you and your team to work more cohesively and efficiently. These tools ensure that everyone is aligned with project goals, reducing delays and enhancing productivity (Tumas, 2024).

To effectively incorporate AI into your writing practices, you should first assess your current content creation workflows to identify areas where AI tools could alleviate bottlenecks or redundancies. Following this assessment, the next step is to select the right AI tools tailored to your specific needs—whether for content generation, editing, or data analysis.

Once integrated, continuous evaluation and feedback loops should be established to measure AI's impact on copywriting efficiency. This involves monitoring output quality, analyzing time savings, and soliciting user feedback to refine your integration strategy. As AI technology continues to evolve, staying abreast of new developments allows you to adapt and optimize your use of AI tools continually.

Content Customization With AI

The significance of tailored content cannot be overstated. t allows you to connect deeply with your audience, fostering engagement and loyalty. AI plays a vital role in this evolution, providing sophisticated tools to enhance personalization at scale.

Natural Language Processing

Natural language processing (NLP) and natural language generation (NLG) are pivotal in crafting messages that resonate with individual preferences, behavior, and emotions. NLP allows computers to understand and interpret human language, enabling more meaningful interactions between your brand and consumers. NLG, on the other hand, is used to produce tailored text automatically, such as product descriptions or marketing emails, ensuring that your messages are relevant and engaging for every recipient.

Data mining and sentiment analysis further augment these capabilities by offering insights into customer behavior and feedback. Thanks to its ability to analyze vast amounts of data, AI can detect patterns and predict future actions, enabling you to deploy personalized campaigns effectively (Winter, 2024). Sentiment analysis helps you understand customer emotions, which is crucial for adjusting your strategies and ensuring that the content not only reaches but also resonates with your target audience.

Personalized Content

Personalized writing isn't just a theoretical benefit for copywriters; it has tangible impacts. Take, for example, the case of Salesforce's Einstein GPT, which leverages AI to create personalized content across various customer touchpoints. This tool enriches customer experiences, leading to higher engagement and conversion rates. Moreover, companies like The Thinking Traveller have demonstrated how AI-driven personalization can significantly boost business outcomes. With their emphasis on customized online experiences, they've witnessed a 33% increase in bookings, illustrating the power of tailoring content to meet specific consumer needs.

The Importance of Human Creativity

Despite the efficiency AI brings, human creativity remains indispensable in creating truly customized experiences. AI can process data and generate content quickly but lacks the emotional intuition and innovativeness inherent in you as a creator (Tumas, 2024). A successful strategy strikes a balance where AI handles data-intensive tasks while you infuse creativity and empathy, crafting messages that genuinely connect on a personal level. This synergy is essential for developing compelling narratives that captivate your audiences.

Moreover, personalized content crafted using AI must navigate ethical considerations. Ensuring transparency in AI usage and respecting data privacy are critical components of ethical marketing practices. You must be transparent about how you use consumer data, maintaining trust and confidence among your audience. You should strive to maintain originality and avoid excessive reliance on AI-generated content to uphold brand integrity.

As technology continues to advance, you must harness AI's potential responsibly, maintaining a delicate balance between automation and creativity. This approach enhances your marketing effectiveness and strengthens your relationships with customers, driving long-term success. The journey towards mastering personalized content through AI is an ongoing process and requires continuous learning and adaptation.

Ethical Considerations in AI Usage

The growing reliance on AI to craft engaging content requires a closer look at how these technologies can be used responsibly. Responsible AI usage involves not only leveraging its capabilities to boost creativity and efficiency but also ensuring that ethical considerations are prioritized in the content creation process.

Transparency and Clear Disclosure

Transparency means declaring upfront when AI is involved (*Navigating Ethical Considerations in AI Writing*, 2024). It serves as a bridge between creators and consumers, fostering transparency that builds lasting trust.

For instance, a company might state on its website or marketing materials exactly how AI contributes to its content strategy. By doing so, it provides consumers with accurate information about its processes, reinforcing credibility and ethical behavior.

Originality

Upholding creativity while avoiding plagiarism and duplication is essential for ethical content generation. AI should assist in brainstorming rather than merely replicating existing ideas (Tiwari, 2023). In addition, it's paramount to take proactive steps to ensure AI-generated content does not inadvertently include plagiarized material. Incorporating plagiarism detection tools into the content creation workflow can further bolster this effort, providing writers with real-time feedback that flags potential issues before publication. Staying aware of the importance of citing sources and respecting intellectual property rights is vital in mitigating any inadvertent ethical breaches.

Accountability

As AI systems generate more content, determining who is responsible—be it the developers, companies, or individuals using the AI—becomes imperative. This multifaceted accountability is essential, especially in light of the potential for inaccuracies, biased information, or even offensive outputs that may arise from AI-generated material.

Should mistakes occur, such as inaccuracies or offensive outputs, having an established framework for accountability ensures swift rectification and minimal reputational damage (Tiwari, 2023). This framework should emphasize the roles and responsibilities, providing guidelines for how each party can take corrective action, whether it includes revising content, issuing public apologies, or implementing changes in AI training protocols to prevent recurrence.

Privacy and Data Protection

Respecting privacy and adhering to data protection regulations remain at the forefront of ethical considerations in AI-assisted copywriting. Compliance with data protection laws is necessary to avoid legal repercussions and uphold consumer privacy rights. It's important to implement robust data handling procedures that ensure all collected information is stored securely and used responsibly within the scope permitted by regulations (*Navigating Ethical Considerations in AI Writing,* 2024).

Moreover, privacy concerns extend to how AI might unknowingly process sensitive information during content generation. Implementing safeguards to prevent the unintentional disclosure of confidential data is crucial. Businesses can employ privacy-preserving techniques in AI training processes to mitigate this risk, ensuring that personal or proprietary information remains protected throughout AI interactions.

The Human Element in AI-driven Copywriting

As artificial intelligence continues to evolve, its role in storytelling has grown, enabling faster content generation with impressive levels of coherence and grammar accuracy. However, despite these advances, one critical element remains beyond AI's reach: genuine creativity and narrative depth.

Creativity

AI technologies excel at analyzing vast data sets and recognizing patterns, which can be beneficial for generating ideas or drafting initial content structures. Yet, these capabilities reveal a significant constraint—AI cannot experience emotions, personal insights, and the nuances of human experiences that enrich storytelling. Creativity involves connecting disparate elements in unique ways, an inherent human capacity driven by intuition and emotional depth. This limitation is captured well in the observation that while AI tools can suggest plot points or generate dialogue, they cannot infuse stories with an authenticity that resonates on a deeper emotional level (Sabba Quidwai, 2024).

Human Intuition

Intuition allows writers to grasp the subtle shifts in tone, character development, and thematic undercurrents that connect with audiences. It brings forth the 'human spark'—the ability to create something genuinely original, reflecting the complexities of life and emotions. This connection between writer and audience is often characterized by empathy and understanding, positioning human writers as vital architects in the storytelling process.

A Collaborative Environment

AI can handle repetitive tasks, perform trend analysis, and offer suggestions, freeing writers to focus more on the creative aspects that require deeper thought and emotional consideration. Encouraging a symbiotic relationship means viewing AI as an assistant rather than a replacement, leveraging its processing abilities while relying on human intuition for final decisions. This partnership can improve efficiency, allowing writers to explore more innovative approaches without being bogged down by routine editorial processes.

One effective way to foster such collaboration is through iterative processes where human feedback refines AI outputs. Writers might start with AI-generated drafts, using these as springboards for more profound thematic exploration. Here, human input ensures the narratives remain rich and layered, avoiding the potential pitfalls of AI's lack of nuanced understanding (Lee, 2024). Techniques like this not only maintain content integrity but also highlight unique human contributions. Hence, t treating AI suggestions as brainstorming aids rather than definitive solutions preserves creative autonomy while reaping the benefits from AI-enhanced productivity.

Quality Control

Human oversight is crucial in ensuring AI-generated content aligns with ethical guidelines and accurately represents desired messages. Reviews involving careful consideration of context, cultural sensitivity, and originality are necessary steps. As machine-generated content becomes more prevalent, establishing comprehensive review protocols helps safeguard against potential errors or biases inherent in AI outputs. This vigilance upholds standards of excellence while protecting brand reputation, making it clear that human involvement is non-negotiable in producing compelling narratives (Lee, 2024).

Summary and Reflections

In this chapter, we've examined the transformative impact of AI on the copywriting landscape. It involves balancing efficiency with personalization and redefining how content is created and customized. We've explored how tools like GPT-3 optimize drafting and enhance creativity, allowing creators to focus on compelling storytelling. At the same time, AI-driven insights help tailor messages that resonate deeply with audiences, supporting a dynamic approach to content strategizing. The discussion also highlighted the significance of ethical considerations, emphasizing transparency, originality, and data privacy to maintain trust in AI-assisted processes.

As we navigate these advancements, it becomes clear that while AI offers remarkable capabilities, the human touch remains indispensable. Effective copywriting in the digital age requires a partnership where AI handles routine tasks, leaving space for human writers to infuse creativity and emotion into their work. This balance ensures they remain at the forefront of delivering engaging, personalized content that resonates with their audience.

Conclusion

As we wrap up this journey into the world of copywriting, let's take a moment to reflect on what we've accomplished together. Whether you're a marketer, business owner, content creator, freelancer, or sales professional, you now have an invaluable toolkit at your disposal. Remember those early pages where we talked about understanding your audience? That foundational skill is going to be crucial as you move forward in refining and adapting these techniques to your specific needs.

You've dug deep into finding the unique voice that resonates with your audience. We touched on crafting irresistible headlines—how they function like magnets for attention—and how effectively crafting your message can mean the difference between someone reading it all the way through or tossing it aside. These basics are your building blocks.

Think back to when we explored storytelling. Remember the power stories have to connect on an emotional level? Consider how brands that tell a compelling story often win not just mindshare but heartshare. It's all about relatability and forging connections that aren't easily forgotten. Don't underestimate the good old emotional appeal—it's timeless and universally effective!

You learned about persuasive techniques, too. Things like social proof, scarcity, and authority are not just buzzwords but strategies that can transform bland copy into a word-of-mouth engine. They turn skeptics into believers and readers into loyal customers.

Throughout your reading, you discovered the nuances of writing clear calls to action. If you've captured attention and built desire, the next natural step is guiding your reader toward action. It's one thing to inform; it's another to convert interest into real, tangible interaction. Your words, when executed properly, hold incredible power—they're your unsung heroes behind every successful conversion.

Let's not forget about the intricacies of editing and revising, either. Precision with words is your secret weapon. Tightening your sentences, cutting excess flab, and keeping things sharp and dialogue-focused— these are your daily drills to ensure your copy stands out.

Now, it's time to put these skills into action. Knowledge without execution is merely potential, so start experimenting! Dive into your work with enthusiasm and be prepared to make mistakes. Every misstep is a lesson wrapped in memory, steering you closer to mastery. Commit to writing a little bit more each day. There will be drafts that make you cringe, but that's okay. Keep pushing forward. Practice isn't just about repetition; it's about consistency and improvement.

Challenge yourself to write outside your comfort zone. Try different styles and aim to surprise your audience with versatility. Play with tones and voices. Ask for feedback. Listen carefully and adapt. Every tweak counts when you're on a pathway toward perfecting your craft.

Here's your homework: Go revamp an old piece of writing using what you've learned, or create something from scratch to integrate these new strategies. Think of it as your project, tailor-made for your growth. Share it with a colleague or friend and invite them to give insight. Use that feedback constructively.

I'd love to hear about your experiences and see how you bring these concepts to life. Share your thoughts, triumphs, and challenges. You'll find immense value in engaging with others who are walking parallel paths—collaborate, innovate, and celebrate together.

Before you go, know this: you have everything it takes to become a masterful copywriter. All it requires is practice, persistence, and passion. The road ahead is paved with possibilities that are yours for the taking.

Thank you for letting me accompany you on this adventure. I hope you feel inspired, equipped, and ready to tackle your next big project. Now, go out there and write copy that doesn't just sell but sings. May your words always find their mark, sparking creativity and conversion wherever they land. Happy writing!

Glossary

A/B Testing: A technique used to compare two versions of a webpage, app, or marketing asset to discover which one is better in terms of performance, user engagement, or conversion rates.

Active Listening: A communication skill that involves fully concentrating, understanding, responding to, and remembering what the other person is saying.

Alliteration: A literary device in which the same initial consonant sound is repeated in closely positioned words or syllables.

Attention, Interest, Desire, and Action (AIDA): A strategy outlining the steps to guide potential customers through the buying process.

Bounce Rate: A web analytics metric measuring the percentage of visitors who enter a website and then leave ("bounce") without viewing any other pages or taking any further action.

Buyer Personas: Semi-fictional models of your ideal buyers based on market research and real data.

Click-Through Rate: A metric used in digital marketing to assess the effectiveness of an online advertising campaign. It represents the ratio of users who click on a specific link compared to the total number of users who view the advertisement.

Call-To-Action (CTA): A prompt in a marketing message that urges the audience to take precise action. It is conceived to provoke an immediate reply or boost a conversion.

Data Mining: The process of uncovering practices, correlations, and useful information from large sets of data.

Feedback Loop: Involves gathering and analyzing responses from readers, customers, or stakeholders to improve the copy.

Fear Of Missing Out (FOMO): A psychological phenomenon where individuals feel anxious that they are missing rewarding or enjoyable experiences that others might be having.

Generative Pre-Trained Transformer (GPT): An artificial intelligence language model created by OpenAI.

Iteration: Refers to the process of repeatedly executing a set of operations or steps in a sequence, often aiming to reach a desired outcome or enhance a solution.

Key Performance Indicators (KPIs): Quantifiable metrics that indicate how effectively an organization, team, or individual is meeting their goals.

Meta-Description: An HTML attribute that offers a concise summary of a web page's content. It usually appears in search engine results pages (SERPs) beneath the page title, helping users understand what the page is about before they click the link.

Meta-Titles: Also known as title tags, these are HTML elements that that define the title of a web page. They are vital for both search engine optimization (SEO) and enhancing user experience.

Mind Mapping: A visual brainstorming tool used to organize information, ideas, or tasks around a central concept. It involves creating a diagram where related ideas branch out from the central idea, forming a structured and hierarchical representation of the information.

Natural Language Generation (NLG): A subfield of artificial intelligence (AI) and natural language processing (NLP) that concentrates on the automated design of human-readable text from data.

Natural Language Processing (NLP): A subfield of artificial intelligence (AI) and linguistics focused on the interaction between computers and humans employing natural language. It concerns the capacity of computers to comprehend, analyze, and develop human language in a way that is both effective and beneficial.

OpenAI: An artificial intelligence study institution that aspires to design and promote friendly AI for the benefit of humanity.

Organic Traffic: Guides visitors who reach your website via unpaid search results.

Psychographics: Refers to the analysis and type of people based on their psychological characteristics, including their values, attitudes, interests, lifestyles, and personality traits.

Return On Investment (ROI): A financial metric used to estimate the profitability or efficiency of an asset.

Segmentation: The strategy of separating a wide target market into smaller, more manageable subgroups based on shared characteristics.

User-Generated Content (UGC): Refers to any form of content—such as text, images, videos, reviews, and social media posts—that is produced and shared by users rather than the brand itself.

Unique Selling Proposition (USP): Refers to a specific characteristic or feature of a product, service, or brand that differentiates it from competitors and makes it particularly appealing to buyers.

Search Behaviors: Refer to the efforts and practices of individuals when they use search engines or other search tools to research information.

Sentiment Analysis: A technique used in natural language processing (NLP) to determine the emotional tone of a piece of text. Its goal is to classify the text as positive, negative, or neutral. Additionally, it may identify specific emotions expressed, such as happiness, anger, or sadness.

Search Engine Optimization (SEO): The practice of optimizing a website or web content to enhance its visibility and ranking on search engine results pages.

Tags: Keywords or labels used to categorize, organize, and identify specific content or elements. They help improve searchability, navigation, and user experience.

User Analytics: Involves the collection, analysis, and interpretation of data concerning user behavior and interactions with a website, application, or digital product. This process offers valuable insights into how users engage with the platform, enabling businesses and organizations to make informed decisions that enhance user experience, optimize performance, and achieve their objectives.

About the Author

Dana Hamilton is a writer with a passion for the art and science of persuasive communication. Drawing on years of experience in business and marketing, Dana distills complex concepts into practical advice that anyone can use. When not writing, Dana enjoys exploring new trends, brainstorming creative ideas, and helping others unlock the power of words. Always curious, Dana believes that great copy isn't just written—it's crafted through a deep understanding of people and what moves them.

References

Abdullah, J. (2024, March 2). *Cultural sensitivity and inclusivity in copywriting: A path to global connection.* Medium. https://medium.com/@support_98349/cultural-sensitivity-and-inclusivity-in-copywriting-a-path-to-global-connection-e48756dd410f

Adam. (2023, July 2). *The power of Cialdini's 6 principles in persuasion.* NetReputation. https://www.netreputation.com/cialdinis-6-principles-of-persuasion/

Agnew, P. (2024, August 6). *8 copywriting hacks backed by science.* HubSpot. https://blog.hubspot.com/marketing/copywriting-insights

Ahmad, J. (2023, June 24). *The role of emotional appeals in copywriting: Connecting on a deeper level.* LinkedIn. https://www.linkedin.com/pulse/role-emotional-appeals-copywriting-connecting-deeper-level-ahmad

Ajao, P. (2023, October 4). *The magic of buyer personas in copywriting.* Medium. https://medium.com/@paul_23986/the-copywriters-ideal-customer-persona-538e5f05a082

Ali, A. (2024, June 17). *How does internal linking help SEO? (How-To + 12 best practices).* HawkSEM. https://hawksem.com/blog/how-does-internal-linking-help-seo/

Analyzing and interpreting data | advertising copywriting class notes. (2024a). Fiveable. https://library.fiveable.me/advertising-copywriting/unit-10/analyzing-interpreting-data/study-guide/LapynH3z2IAwzYzN

Ashley. (2024, January 30). *Cut the jargon, boost satisfaction: Why plain language matters in customer experience.* REI Systems. https://www.reisystems.com/cut-the-jargon-boost-satisfaction-why-plain-language-matters-in-customer-experience/

Aw, B. (2024, February 7). *How to do copywriting research: My 7-step guide for creators.* Brendan Aw. https://brendanaw.com/copywriting-research

Bernazzani, S. (2017, October 10). *Intrinsic and extrinsic motivation: What's the difference?* Hubspot. https://blog.hubspot.com/marketing/intrinsic-and-extrinsic-motivation

Bhavya Sri Khandrika. (2024, October 6). *Why writers need feedback to succeed (and you should too)?* Medium. https://medium.com/@bhavya-sri-khandrika/why-writers-need-feedback-to-succeed-and-you-should-too-b0e757bc508b

Bishop, C. (2024, March 21). *Customer trust: Definition, importance & 5 ways to gain it.* Zendesk. https://www.zendesk.com/blog/customer-trust/

Botta, A. (2024). *10 tips for constructive creative and copy feedback.* Bynder. https://www.bynder.com/en/blog/ten-tips-for-constructive-creative-copy-feedback/

Bray, P. (2022, April 4). *How to analyze your competitors effectively [2024].* Mouseflow. https://mouseflow.com/blog/competitive-strategy-how-to-analyze-your-competitors-in-2022/

Breaux, M. (2021). *5 tools to turn copywriting into data-driven copywriting.* Anyword.com. https://www.anyword.com/blog/5-tools-data-driven-copywriting

Brebion, A. (2018, June 27). *5 clever scarcity and urgency examples to boost your conversions.* AB Tasty. https://www.abtasty.com/blog/scarcity-urgency-marketing/

Brosch, R. (2018). What we "see" when we read: Visualization and vividness in reading fictional narratives. *Cortex, 105,* 135–143. https://doi.org/10.1016/j.cortex.2017.08.020

Carmicheal, K. (2021, December 30). *Features vs. benefits: A crash course on proper messaging.* Hubspot. https://blog.hubspot.com/marketing/features-vs-benefits-messaging-ht

Chakraborty, P. (2023, November 4). *The role of analytics in refining your content strategy.* Winsavvy. https://www.winsavvy.com/role-of-analytics-in-refining-your-content-strategy/

Chow, M. (2022, March 14). *What are psychographics? How they make your copy better.* Copyhackers. https://copyhackers.com/2022/03/what-are-psychographics/

Clickable. (2023, December 3). *Rational appeal: The power of logic in persuasion strategies.* Clickable Agency. https://clickable.agency/rational-appeal-exploring-the-power-of-logic-in-persuasion-strategies/

Copywriting skills: Master the art of crafting clickworthy content. (2023c, June 20). Copywriting.org. https://copywriting.org/copywriting-skills/

Creating stories that stick: The psychology of effective storytelling in marketing. (2023, December 27). Blue Monarch Group. https://bluemonarchgroup.com/blog/creating-stories-that-stick-the-psychology-of-effective-storytelling-in-marketing/

Dennison, K. (2023, April 13). *The importance of upskilling and continuous learning in 2023.* Forbes. https://www.forbes.com/sites/karadennison/2023/04/13/the-importance-of-upskilling-and-continuous-learning-in-2023/

Doan, D. (2023, June 29). *How to conduct a competitor analysis — the complete guide.* Hubspot. https://blog.hubspot.com/marketing/seo-competitor-analysis

Dobre, E. (2013, December 9). *Best practices for optimizing call to action buttons.* Omniconvert. https://www.omniconvert.com/blog/call-to-action-optimization-for-online-conversions/

Dogli Wilberforce. (2023, April 16). *9 simple techniques to address customers' pain points: Empathy-driven selling.* The Orange Journal. https://medium.com/the-orange-journal/9-simple-techniques-to-address-customers-pain-points-empathy-driven-selling-cd3630d5f44e

Dutta, A. (2023, August 30). *What is audience segmentation and why it's important?* Revnew. https://revnew.com/blog/what-is-audience-segmentation

Edwards, K. (2024, October 2). *Scarcity marketing secrets: How top brands create urgency and drive sales.* Keegan Edwards. https://keeganedwards.com/scarcity-marketing-secrets-how-top-brands-create-urgency-and-drive-sales/

Farber, N. (2020, December 8). *The psychology of successful copywriting | psychology today.* Psychology Today. https://www.psychologytoday.com/us/blog/the-blame-game/202012/the-psychology-successful-copywriting

Goyette, K. (2019, September 10). *StackPath.* Industry Week. https://www.industryweek.com/leadership/article/22028209/six-motivational-drivers-and-how-to-unleash-them

Grigat, W. (2022, August 19). *A-b-testing-advertising-copy-copywriter-collective.* Copywriter Collective. https://copywritercollective.com/a-b-testing-advertising-copy/

Haim, I. (2023, January 14). *800+ power words: The secret of successful copy revealed!* Elementor. https://elementor.com/blog/power-words/

Hall, D. (2024, July 10). *KPIs for copywriters: Measure success and optimize your performance! - creativewriting-prompts.com.* Creative Writing. https://www.creativewriting-prompts.com/copywriting/kpis-for-copywriters-measure-success-and-optimize-your-performance/

Hardwick, J. (2019, May 30). *Search intent: The overlooked "ranking factor" you should be optimizing for in 2019.* Ahrefs. https://ahrefs.com/blog/search-intent/

Hardwick, J. (2020, February 5). *Meta tags for SEO: A simple guide for beginners.* Ahrefs. https://ahrefs.com/blog/seo-meta-tags/

Harrison, K. (2023, June 1). *Workplace audience segmentation is important for better communication.* Cutting Edge PR. https://cuttingedgepr.com/articles/workplace-audience-segmentation-important-better-communication/

Hicks, K. (2020, September 21). *How to use statistics in your content marketing writing.* Austin Copywriter. https://austin-copywriter.com/how-to-use-statistics-in-your-content-marketing-writing/

How to connect features to benefits: How to sell more effectively. (2023b, March 30). Copywriting.org. https://copywriting.org/how-to-connect-features-to-benefits/

How to increase customer perceived value: 13 psychology-backed strategies. (2024, January 19). WordStream. https://www.wordstream.com/blog/ws/2022/12/21/customer-perceived-value

How to research for copywriting like a pro: Uncover the secrets. (2023a, March 9). Copywriting.org. https://copywriting.org/how-to-research-for-copywriting/

How to use mind mapping for effective brainstorming. (n.d.). Atlassian. https://www.atlassian.com/team-playbook/plays/mind-mapping

How to write attention-grabbing headlines: 14 strategies. (2021, March 30). Forbes. https://www.forbes.com/councils/forbescommunicationscouncil/2021/03/30/how-to-write-attention-grabbing-headlines-14-strategies/

Hurley Hall, S. (2018, March 26). *SEO made simple: Where & how to use keywords in your content.* OptinMonster. https://optinmonster.com/using-keywords-to-improve-your-seo/

Internal linking — SEO best practices 2020. (n.d.). Moz. https://moz.com/learn/seo/internal-link

Ioffe, A., & Borstch. (2023, November 22). *Exploring The Use of Anchoring in Marketing Text.* Borstch. https://borstch.com/blog/copywriting/exploring-the-use-of-anchoring-in-marketing-text

Iterating and refining copy based on performance | advertising copywriting class notes. (2024b). Fiveable. https://library.fiveable.me/advertising-copywriting/unit-10/iterating-refining-copy-based-performance/study-guide/WpGhxhmxu9z4rrXh

Jamal, T. (2024, February 2). *Learn how to use problem-solving skills to craft catchy, clear, and relevant headlines for your articles. discover the steps, techniques, and tools to improve your headline writing.* LinkedIn. https://www.linkedin.com/advice/3/how-can-you-use-problem-solving-skills-improve-article-7v7gc

Johnson, A. (2024, August 20). *SEO keyword research: What it is and why it's important for SEO.* Clearscope. https://www.clearscope.io/blog/what-is-keyword-research-in-SEO

King, D. (2019, May 8). *23 tested methods for crafting the perfect headline [webinar].* Brafton. https://www.brafton.com/blog/strategy/23-tested-methods-for-crafting-the-perfect-headline-webinar/

Kolowich, L. (2018). *How to do A/B testing: A checklist you'll want to bookmark.* Hubspot. https://blog.hubspot.com/marketing/how-to-do-a-b-testing

Krunal Vaghasiya. (2024, October 16). *12 conversion copywriting tips with example to grow sales.* Wisernotify. https://wisernotify.com/?p=31586

Kucukural, N. (2023, February 14). *3 real-life examples of successful storytelling in copywriting.* The Startup. https://medium.com/swlh/3-real-life-examples-of-successful-storytelling-in-copywriting-db67794d1329

Lee. (2023, November 2). *How to use open loops in copywriting (with examples).* The Copy Brothers. https://thecopybrothers.com/blog/how-to-use-open-loops-in-copywriting-with-examples/

Lee, M. (2024, March 12). *AI personalization: 5 examples + business challenges.* Bloomreach. https://www.bloomreach.com/en/blog/ai-personalization-5-examples-business-challenges

Lua, A. (2017, May 2). *Social proof: What it is and 18 ways to use it in your marketing.* Buffer Library. https://buffer.com/library/social-proof/

Maku Seun. (2023, September 22). *How to improve sales by A/B testing your copy.* Maku Seun. https://makucopywriter.com/a-b-testing/

Maku Seun. (2024, May 13). *How to address your customer's pain points in copywriting.* Maku Seun. https://makucopywriter.com/how-to-address-customer-pain-points-with-copywriting/

McCormick, K. (2024, January 19). *26 brilliant ways to use psychology in copywriting (+examples).* WordStream. https://www.wordstream.com/blog/ws/2021/09/01/psychology-copywriting-tips-examples

McFarland, J. (2024, June 18). *Why compelling language in your call to action is a must.* Women Conquer Business. https://www.womenconquerbiz.com/compelling-calls-to-action/

Navigating ethical considerations in AI writing. (2024). B12. https://www.b12.io/resource-center/ai-how-to-guides/navigating-ethical-considerations-in-ai-writing.html

O'Connell, O. (2023, August 14). *Five core elements of paid social ad copywriting.* NoGood™: Growth Marketing Agency. https://nogood.io/2023/08/14/paid-social-ad-copywriting/

Oladipo, T. (2022, June 6). *User generated content: What it is and how to use it.* Buffer Resources. https://buffer.com/resources/what-is-user-generated-content/

Pascoe, R. S. (2024, June 14). *The power of scarcity in copywriting: How to create a sense of urgency - top direct response copywriter for hire.* Top Direct Response Copywriter for Hire. https://worldclasscopywriting.com/the-power-of-scarcity-in-copywriting/

Patel, N. (2022, August 17). *5 ways to use Google Trends for SEO.* Neil Patel. https://neilpatel.com/blog/google-trends-marketing/

The power of branding in website copywriting. (2023, September 11). AIContentfy. https://aicontentfy.com/en/blog/power-of-branding-in-website-copywriting

Rao, A. (2023, July 20). *What is market segmentation? Definition, 5 types, and examples.* LogRocket Blog. https://blog.logrocket.com/product-management/market-segmentation-definition-5-types-examples/

Saad , S. S. (2024, May 29). *Constructive critique: Mastering feedback for personal growth - wide impact.* Wide Impact. https://wide-impact.com/blog/constructive-critique-mastering-feedback-for-personal-growth/

Sabba Quidwai. (2024, July 8). *The last screenwriter: The collaborative conflict between AI and human creativity - designing schools with Dr. Sabba Quidwai.* Designing Schools. https://designingschools.org/the-last-screenwriter-the-collaborative-conflict-between-ai-and-human-creativity/

Sellers, A. (2022, February 4). *The AIDA model: A proven framework for converting strangers into customers.* Hubspot. https://blog.hubspot.com/marketing/aida-model

6 SEO writing essentials: How we craft content that ranks. (2024, July 8). Growth Machine. https://www.growthmachine.com/blog/seo-writing

Slade, H. (2023, March 7). *Storytelling copywriting: How to use it + top formulas.* Slade Copy House. https://sladecopyhouse.com/storytelling-copywriting/

Stillgoe, D. (2024, June 13). *What is a website call-to-action (CTA)? Examples and best practices.* Blendb2b. https://www.blendb2b.com/blog/website-call-to-action-cta-examples-and-best-practices

Strategic call-to-action (CTA) placement for local business websites. (2024, April 20). BuzzBoard. https://www.buzzboard.ai/strategic-call-to-action-cta-placement-for-local-business-websites/

Telci, E. E., Maden, C., & Kantur, D. (2011). The theory of cognitive dissonance: A marketing and management perspective. *Procedia - Social and Behavioral Sciences, 24*(1), 378–386. https://doi.org/10.1016/j.sbspro.2011.09.120

Testimonial vs review: Strategies for building trust, loyalty, and brand reputation through customer testimonial and reviews. (2024). Testimonialdonut.com. https://www.testimonialdonut.com/resources/testimonial-vs-review-strategies-for-building-trust-loyalty-and-brand-reputation

Thoughtlab. (n.d.). *The art of emotional appeal: Creating copy that resonates with your target audience.* Thoughtlab. https://www.thoughtlab.com/blog/the-art-of-emotional-appeal-creating-copy-that-resonates/

Tiên Nguyễn. (2014, September 9). *Four editors give tips on writing headlines. you won't believe what happens next.* The Open Notebook. https://www.theopennotebook.com/2014/09/09/writing-headlines/

Tiwari, A. (2023, December 6). *Ethical considerations in ai-generated content creation.* Content Bloom. https://contentbloom.com/blog/ethical-considerations-in-ai-generated-content-creation/

Tumas, A. (2024). *Exploring the value: Is AI copywriting truly worth it?* Ocoya. https://www.ocoya.com/blog/ai-copywriting-value

Ud-deen, H. (2020, May 5). *6 neurolinguistics and NLP principles to power up your copy.* CXL. https://cxl.com/blog/6-neurolinguistics-principles-to-power-up-your-copy/

Vahid Bakhtvar, & Piri, M. (2021). Investigating the effect of celebrity endorsement on brand credibility, corporate credibility, advertising credibility, consumer social status on buy intention. *National Conference on New Achievements in Management, Economics and Accounting Research.* https://www.researchgate.net/publication/354527568_Investi gating_the_effect_of_celebrity_endorsement_on_brand_credib ility_corporate_credibility_advertising_credibility_consumer_so cial_status_on_buy_intention

Wells, R. (2023, September 4). *Active listening skills: What they are and why they're important.* Forbes. https://www.forbes.com/sites/rachelwells/2023/09/04/active -listening-skills-what-they-are-and-why-theyre-important/

Winter, T. (2024, August 12). *AI copywriting techniques: The secret to engaging content.* SEOwind. https://seowind.io/ai-copywriting-techniques/

Yan, R., Myers, C., Wang, J., & Ghose, S. (2014). Bundling products to success: The influence of complementarity and advertising. *Journal of Retailing and Consumer Services, 21*(1), 48–53. https://doi.org/10.1016/j.jretconser.2013.07.007

Made in United States
Orlando, FL
13 April 2025

60472025R00105